Sanjan Excavation Report Volume 3

Early Medieval Sanjan

Aspects and analysis

Sharad Rajaguru
Sushama Deo
Pramod Joglekar
Padmakar Prabhune
Vijay Sathe
Shivendra Kadgaonkar
Arati Deshpande-Mukherjee

BAR International Series 2509
2013

Published in 2016 by
BAR Publishing, Oxford

BAR International Series 2509

Sanjan Excavation Report Volume 3
Series Editors: Dr S. P. Gupta (deceased), Dr Homi Dhalla and Mr K. N. Dikshit

Early Medieval Sanjan

ISBN 978 1 4073 1127 2

BAR Publishing is the trading name of British Archaeological Reports (Oxford) Ltd.
British Archaeological Reports was first incorporated in 1974 to publish the BAR
Series, International and British. In 1992 Hadrian Books Ltd became part of the BAR
group. This volume was originally published by Archaeopress in conjunction with
British Archaeological Reports (Oxford) Ltd / Hadrian Books Ltd, the Series principal
publisher, in 2013. This present volume is published by BAR Publishing, 2016.

Printed in England

BAR
PUBLISHING

BAR titles are available from:

BAR Publishing
122 Banbury Rd, Oxford, OX2 7BP, UK
EMAIL   info@barpublishing.com
PHONE   +44 (0)1865 310431
FAX   +44 (0)1865 316916
www.barpublishing.com

TABLE OF CONTENTS

Foreword   iii

Medieval Sanjan: A Geomorphological Background   1
Sushama G. Deo and S.N. Rajaguru

Faunal Remains from Sanjan, District Valsad, Gujarat   11
P.P. Joglekar

Catalogue of Coins from the Excavations at Sanjan (Umbargaon Taluka, District Valsad, Gujarat)   37
Padmakar Prabhune
Vijay Sathe

A Report on the Sculptures from Sanjan, 2004   59
Shivendra B. Kadgaonkar

A Report on the Molluscan Shell Remains from Sanjan Excavations (2002-2004)   67
Arati Deshpande-Mukherjee

i

FOREWORD

The World Zarathushti Cultural Foundation (WZCF) was established by Dr. Homi Dhalla in 1998 for the promotion and preservation of Zoroastrian culture. Being deeply interested in Zoroastrian history, he thought it imperative to launch a project which would throw light on the early history of the Parsis. With this in mind, one of the first major projects he embarked upon was the excavation at Sanjan.

Thus the Sanjan excavations were undertaken under the auspices of the WZCF in collaboration with the Indian Archaeological Society (IAS), New Delhi, between 2002 and 2004. Late Dr. S. P. Gupta, Chairman of IAS, was the Director of Excavations, providing guidance and direction to the project with his rich experience and expertise, until his unfortunate demise in 2007. Dr. Gupta recognized the immense importance and relevance of the Sanjan project, not only for understanding Parsi history, but also for the study of Medieval archaeology in India. It is with some pride that WZCF and IAS can claim to have broken new ground and to have conducted the first Early Medieval excavations in India. This is a period of history that has been quite neglected in Indian archaeology. The Sanjan excavations have generated interest and opened up a whole new approach in the discipline, so that several projects focusing on Indian Ocean trade and the Early Medieval period are now being undertaken by archaeologists and historians in India. The excavations at Sanjan (2002–2004) were undertaken as part of this endeavour and were financed by the Indian Council of Historical Research, the Archaeological Survey of India and Sir Dorabji Tata Trust through the WZCF.

It is with immense pleasure that the WZCF and IAS present the present volume, the third in the excavation report series. The first volume consisted of the ceramics report and the second on human remains. This volume adds to the huge amount of information and data generated by the excavations and explorations undertaken between 2002 and 2004. The WZCF and IAS are deeply appreciative of the efforts made by several specialists and scientists to study different aspects of the site and to contribute their reports for inclusion in this volume.

Reports on the geo-morphology of the area, animal bones, shells, coins and iconography are included in this volume. It is hoped they will add new dimensions to the information on Sanjan and provide a more holistic picture of this ancient settlement.

The relevance of Sanjan as an active participant in the commerce of the Indian Ocean and the nature of the settlement as a port town on the west coast of India, have been largely defined by its location and the geology of the area. Profs. Sharad Rajaguru and Sushama Deo explored and surveyed the entire estuarine area of Sanjan, Nargol and Umbargam in 2004. Their report places the settlement of Sanjan in perspective. Prof. Pramod Joglekar's study of the large collection of animal bones found during the excavations and their distribution patterns is extremely important in identifying both wild as well as domestic species. Dr. Arati Deshpande-Mukherjee's study of the shells found in the excavations adds to the rich database for the site. Dr. Padmakar Prabhune and Dr. Vijay Sathe have done an admirable job of cataloguing and analysing the coins found in the excavations and from the surface. Some of these are extremely rare and a few are unique samples which have not been reported from any other site before. Not only do these provide a chronological framework to the site, they are also invaluable in recreating and understanding the economic profile of Sanjan. Equally relevant in corroborating other excavated data is Dr. Shivendra Kadgaonkar's survey and documentation of the sculptures found at Sanjan. Most of these belong to the Rashtrakuta period.

WZCF and IAS are indeed happy to place these findings on record so that scholars working in this field may benefit from the information that has come to light.

Dr. Homi Dhalla
World Zarathushti Cultural Foundation,
Mumbai, India

Mr. K. N. Dikshit
Indian Archaeological Society,
New Delhi, India

MEDIEVAL SANJAN:
A GEOMORPHOLOGICAL BACKGROUND

Sushama G. Deo and S.N. Rajaguru

Introduction

The western coast of India, to the south of river Tapi is primarily rocky. It lacks true deltas and is flanked by the Western Ghats with humid tropical climate where the rainfall varies from 3000 mm in south to about 1800 mm per year in the northern part. The streams originating on the western scarp of the Western Ghats, are short (~ 40 km) and flow through narrow gorge like valleys developed in the pre-Cambrian rocks, Deccan Traps of the Cretaceous-Eocene age and the laterites of the Late Tertiary age. There is no evidence of any major marine transgression with deep water marine facies during the entire Quaternary. These short streams have typical fluvial environment in the upper reaches and are dominated by fluvio-marine environment in their estuarine portion (lower reaches). The estuarine part of the river is affected by strong monsoonal freshwater inflow for about four months (June-September), by tidal processes in the remaining eight months and also by strong wind activity for four months (April to July). These estutaries are sometimes affected by catastrophic monsoon floods and by very strong tides at times related to earthquakes.

Archaeologically, the coastal region has preserved primary and secondary sites which range in culture from Lower Palaeolithic to the Medieval. Number of Palaeolithic sites has been reported since the early of part of 20th century. These studies reveal that late Acheulian site occurs in rubble sediments in natural cave deposit within the laterite near Guhagar Marathe (2004), while Middle Palaeolithic workshop sites occurs within the tidal zone on a rocky bench near Malvan (Guzder 1980). Joshi and Bopardikar (1972) excavated the Mesolithic site in a primary context in the cave at Hatkhamba near Ratnagiri. Number of Upper Palaeolithic and Mesolithic sites have been reported around Mumbai and north of it (Todd 1939; Sankalia 1962; Malik 1963). However, none of these Stone Age sites have been securely dated due to lack of reliable datable material.

On the other hand archaeology of the Mid to Late Holocene period is receiving better attention by archaeologists and scientists. Recently scholars from Deccan College have used multidisciplinary approach to study late Holocene sites at Chaul, Sopara and Kelshi. These sites occur within 2 to 3 km from the coast and are associated with littoral sediments. Ghate's (1985, 1988) multi-disciplinary studies showed that Sopara was never a port on the open sea but operated as a creek port all throughout the historical period.

During the Early Historic times, Sopara was situated on an island surrounded by creeks. The two islands got connected due to silting in the late 18th century (Ghate 1990). Owing to continuous silting with sediments, Sopara seized to be functional and probably lost its importance. Recent geoarchaeological investigations at Kelshi (Deo *et al.* 2001, Joglekar *et al.* 2001-02) indicate that anthropogenic activity has taken place during decreased level of sand accumulation. The rate of sand accumulation is controlled by wind speed, wind direction, long exposure of suitable sand size material for blowing and vegetation or other barriers to trap the sand. Changes in the intensity of sand accumulation at Kelshi is partly connected with slight rise and fall in sea level which is also related to global climatic factors as observed recently by Anderson *et al.* (2002) and Gupta *et al.* (2003). Both these studies have shown that configurational changes in the estuarine zone are dominant. Gogte (2004) found archaeological evidence in semi-primary context at Chaul and recorded not only the Satvahana pottery but also ring-wells, coins, saddle querns, glass beads and bangles of that period at several places on the old mud flat of the Kundalika river. An ancient embankment wall and a dilapidated stone structure resembling a jetty have been located on the edges of the old mud flat. This study has thrown good light on maritime trade during the Satvahana period.

This brief review of investigations carried out by various scholars reveal complex nature of man-land relationships during the Quaternary (late Pleistocene and mid-late Holocene) in a non-deltaic rocky coastline of Western India. On this background the Medieval site at Sanjan provides additional information on Late Holocene environmental changes and settlement related to the arrival of the Parsi community in India.

Location and Physical Environment

The Medieval site at Sanjan is located 2.5 km inland from the present mouth of the river Varoli. The river Varoli originates at 20 km southeast of Sanjan in the hill ranges (150-200 m) in district Thane, Maharashtra. It is a rocky stream and flows through a 10-15 m deep gorge in its middle course. The course of this river is east-west in the upper reaches. However, it takes an abrupt turn and flows south-north as almost a straight course for 3.5 km indicating probable north-south lineament control. In the lower reaches (estuarine zone, i.e. from its mouth near Umbergaon

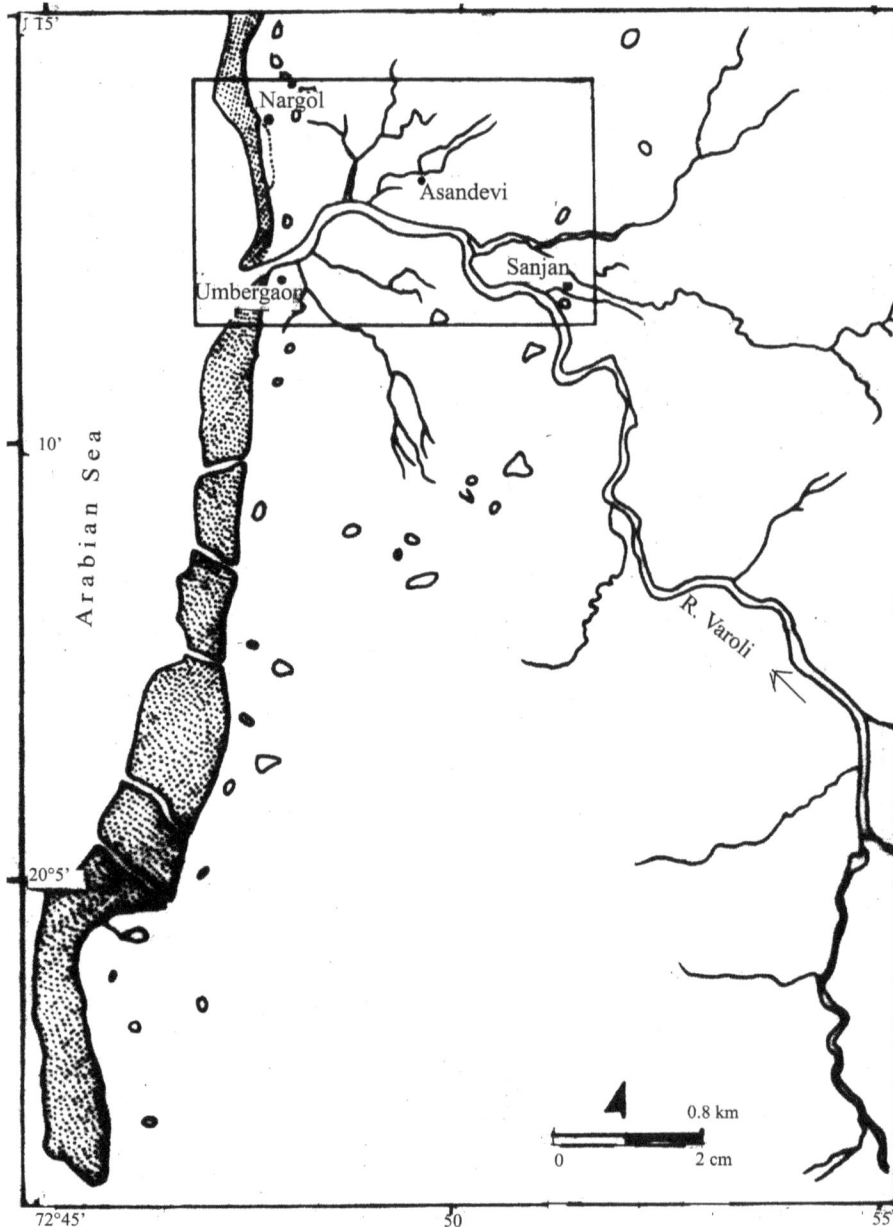

Fig.1. Location Map

to Railway station) it again changes to east-west trend. The river is tidal for 6 to 7 km upstream and drains a flat alluvial fill surface of 10-15 m thickness (Fig.1).

Field Observations

A reconnaissance field survey of the exposed sections from the mouth of the river Varoli to 5 km upstream of it was carried out. These field observations provide background geomorphic data for the Medieval site of Sanjan. Recently, Rajaguru and Deo (2005) have given a preliminary report on the coastal geomorphology of Sanjan. The hard rocks exposed in the area belong to varieties of basalt of the Cretaceous-Eocene Age. These rocks are unconformably covered by thin (less than 10 m) surficial sediments of fluvial and littoral origin. Some of the well-exposed sections on the river Varoli and its tributaries have been studied in detail, and following four major lithological units have been observed (Table 1.)

Unit I Beach-Dune complex rocks 'karal'

Normally, beach rock is defined as a lithological unit developed in inter-tidal zone and consists of marine shell fragments, sands and pebbles. Guzder (1980) observed that beach rock traditionally labeled as 'littoral concrete' is of complex origin, i.e. it has formed in the beach and dune environment. She, therefore, coined a locally used term 'karal' for these rocks. The same term has been used in the present communication. The 'karal' is well-laminated rock and is cemented by calcitic cement. It was well-investigated by Guzder (1980), Ghate (1988), Chamyal and Mehr (1995) and Bruckner (2001). Guzder (1980) dated number of 'karal' rocks by radiocarbon method and these dates range from 4245 to 1110 yrs B.P. As these dates are on the whole rock samples, they therefore, indicate the minimum ages. Ghate (1988) has made comparative study of radiocarbon dates obtained on 'karal' and driftwood found in the same section at Sopara. She showed that the

Table 1. The lithological units in and around Sanjan

Lithological unit	Location and thickness	Approximate age, with Cultural material if any
Unit I Beach-dune complex rock locally known as 'karal'	Nargol – 8 m Two generations of beach-dune complex Umbergaon – 4m	Late Quaternary Holocene
Unit II Alluvial fills	Asan Devi – 6 m Calcretised Dara – 5 m Non-calcretised	Late Pleistocene Late Holocene Medieval pottery
Unit III Mud flats	Sanjan – 4 m Excavated site	Mid to Late Holocene Medieval pottery
Unit IV Sandbar Defunct lakes/ponds	Nargol Agar to Saronda	Modern sandbar Late Holocene (?)

'karal' date is younger than the date obtained on wood by several hundred years. Whatever may be the nature of dates on 'karal', one can argue that these rocks are of Mid to Late Holocene in ages and have developed in response to minor sea level changes within the amplitude of couple of meters of the present sea level. Against this brief background of geomorphic significance of 'karal', two exposures of 'karal' around Sanjan have been described here.

a. Umbergaon:

The 'karal' at Umbergaon is about 4 m thick and occurs within the present nip tide. It is well-laminated, with a westerly dip of about 25° and has developed solution cavities, a result of karstic weathering (Fig. 2). The 'Umbergaon' outcrop occurs as an isolated outcrop within the mud flat. Chamyal and Mehr (1995:249) have mentioned this outcrop as linear patches (100-150 m long and 10 m wide) and are located at 10 m above the high water line. They found that these rocks are similar to those of Saurashtra and in addition to molluscan shell fragments, contain foraminifera like *Ratalia*, *Ammonia*, etc. They have placed this beach rock within the Holocene, without giving any absolute date.

b. Nargol

The 'karal' outcrop at Nargol is well-exposed in a quarry section. It is 8 m thick and has preserved a two-tire stratigraphy (Fig. 3). The basal 'karal' is capped by 30-40 cm thick blackish sand, probably rich in magnetite and illmenite and is moderately cemented by calcium carbonate. The black sand layer grades into well-laminated moderately consolidated shell rich sand. This shelly sand further grades to well-sorted brownish sand with a thickness of 70 cm. This brownish sand has also developed distinct blocky peds, thereby suggesting that the brownish layer represent palaeosol developed over 'karal' during a phase of non-deposition in response to recession of sea. This palaeosol is capped by 2 m thick well-sorted sand that is weakly pedogenised as indicated

by loss of lamination and by presence of karstic solution cavities in the upper part. The 'karal' at Nargol represents two generations of beach-dune complex rocks as indicated by a development of brownish palaeosol at a depth of 2 m below the stabilised surface of the 'karal' ridge (Fig. 4).

On the basis of degree of weathering, the 'karal' ridge at Nargol is considered to be relatively older than that of Umbergaon. Both these ridges occur as isolated outcrops surrounded by well-developed mud flats (Unit III) and have formed in response to transgressive-regressive phases of sea during the Holocene.

Unit II *Alluvial fills*

The second unit consisted of alluvial fills of river Varoli observed at Asan Devi and Dara villages.

Asan Devi

An isolated outcrop of the calcretised alluvial fill (5-6 m thick) above the modern mud flat occurs as an island near Asan Devi village (Fig. 5). This alluvium consists of yellowish to reddish sandy silt, which is strongly affected by pedogenic and groundwater calcrete. The modern mud flat is inset into the older alluvial flat of river Varoli. Presence of calcrete in the alluvial fill suggests relative degree of aridity during the Last Glacial Maximum (LGM) period when the summer monsoon was weak and the sea level was low. Thus, the alluvial fill preserved at Asan Devi village is a relict fluvial landform of the Late Pleistocene age.

Dara

Another interesting example of alluvial fill terrace is observed near Dara village on the left bank of a small tributary (Tukkar nala) of river Varoli (Fig. 6). This place is beyond present tidal effect and is about 3 km upstream of Sanjan site. The alluvial fill is 5 m thick

Fig.2. Karal at Umbergaon

Fig.3. Karal at Nargol

Fig.4. Section showing details of Beach-dune complex indicating two generations of transgression-regression at Nargol

and laterally extends about 1 km. It consists of non-calcereous brownish sandy silt, crudely laminated, with thin bands of loose sands. The silt rests on cross-bedded sandy- pebbly gravel, which is about 1.5 m thick. The silt has preserved charcoal fragments, potsherds and also burnt clay lumps.

The same sandy-silty deposit has also been seen in the excavated trenches at Sanjan. Also on the periphery of the Sanjan site a rubble-like deposit consisting of washed potsherds and other cultural material is found to be associated with the sandy-silty deposit.

Both these alluvial fill sections (near Asan Devi and Dara) indicate strong monsoon floods, which have disturbed part of the Sanjan habitation during 13-14th century.

Unit III *Mud flats*

Mud flats (also known as tidal flats) are always found next to salt marshes. Twice each day, water flows in and out with the tides, filling or draining the flat. Mud flat coastlines occur only where the shore is protected from waves. This may be found where a river meets the ocean and a sand spit has formed across the entrance. The entire area is called an estuary if the freshwater flow is slow and the ocean flows into the river mouth - in with each high tide and out at the low tide. The gentle movement of saltwater inland brings

fine sediments and the slow movement of the river also brings fine sediments. These fine sediments settle out as mud. At low tide this inter-tidal mud is exposed as a mud flat leaving water only in the permanent channels. At high tide the mud flat is covered with water.

The occupation site of Sanjan is situated on gently rolling landscape developed on mud flat –younger than beach-dune ridge and also than the calcretised alluvial fill of the Late Pleistocene/ Early Holocene age. Our examination of exposed cliff section close to Sanjan revealed that the transported pottery occurs as rubble in silty alluvium throughout for 2 to 3 m (Fig. 7). It is therefore, suggested that the site has been affected by flood erosion on its peripheral part. Proper radiocarbon dating of the flood silt with pottery could add new information on site modification due to natural processes operating in the estuarine zone.

Unit IV *Sand bar and Defunct ponds*

There is well-developed modern sand bar at the mouth of Varoli near Nargol (Fig. 8). The modern beach at Nargol is comparatively coarser dominated with basalt pebbles and shells. Few weathered potsherds were found from this beach.

From the topographic sheet (46 D/16- surveyed in 1884-85) an interesting feature has been noted, i.e. the presence of small lake/ponds along the coast. There is a series of ponds

Fig.5. Calcretised alluvial fill at Asan Devi

Fig.6. Non-calcretised alluvium at Dara with potsherds and charcoal

Fig.7. Exposed cliff section at Sanjan showing transported cultural remains

from Agar in the south and to Saronda in the north (Fig. 1). These ponds are located 0.5 to 1 km inland from the coast. This feature indicates recession of sea from the lake-line to the present-day coast. For further understanding of the palaeogeography of the area detailed geomorphological investigations and dating are required.

Summary

Geomorphological observations made around Sanjan have brought out some new features related to environmental changes for the first time. It appears that strongly calcretised alluvial fills, which today occur as relict landforms, have developed during the relatively dry climatic phase of the late Pleistocene when sea level was also low by several meters. Documentation of relative degree of aridity in the present sub-humid parts of Sanjan confirms similar observations made in the sub-humid/humid parts of North Konkan (Ghate 1985), West Bengal (Basak 1997), Meghalaya (Sharma 2001) and Manipur (Thokchom 1987).

Beach-dune complex ('karal') ridges at Umbergaon and Nargol represent at least three transgressive-regressive phases of Early to Mid Holocene (less than 7000 yrs B.P.). It also partially supports earlier studies carried out by Guzder (1980) and Ghate (1985) in Konkan coast and by Chamyal and Mehr (1995) in south Gujarat. These studies have also brought out one important factor i.e.

configurational changes responsible for development of near coastal landforms. Such changes involve catastrophic floods, unusual high tides, landslides in the catchment area, sudden changes in the sediment–water budget in the estuarine zone and cyclonic storms and tsunamis related to earthquakes. Recently it has been realised that the problem of sea level changes on coasts of Konkan and Gujarat is complex. It is, therefore, not easy to prepare a simple curve of sea level changes in the last 10,000 (Mathur 2005).

We suggest that the estuarine zone around Sanjan has been affected by moderate sea level fluctuations and by coastal configurational changes. Such changes are seen in the form of catastrophic monsoonal floods, development of sand bar at the mouth of the creek and sudden variation in transportation of silt/clay load due to complex relationship between fluvial and marine processes operating in a humid monsoonal estuary.

In this short communication it has been possible to provide basic framework of geomorphic features around Sanjan. The observations need to be verified in future fieldwork at Sanjan, Dahanu and Palgarh and by well-supported radiocarbon dates. Hence, we propose to have long-term geomorphic field studies in future to understand natural factors responsible for the growth and decay of the Medieval Parsi settlements in South Gujarat.

Fig.8. Recent sand bar development at Nargol

Acknowledgments

We gratefully acknowledge Dr. Kurush Dalal for inviting us to attend the excavation at Sanjan and for arranging field trip around Sanjan for geomorphological work. We thank Dr. Dhalla for his help in this work.

References:

Anderson, David, M., J.T. Overpack and Anil Gupta. 2002. Increase in the Asian Southwest Monsoon during the Past Four Centuries, *Science* 297:596-599.

Basak Bishnupriya 1997. Prehistoric Settlement Patterns of the Tara Feni Valley, Midnapur District, West Bengal. Unpublished Ph.D. Dissertation, Pune: University of Poona.

Bruckner H.M. 2001. Late Quaternary Shorelines in India. In: Gunnell, Y. and B.P. Radhakrishna (Eds.) *Sahyadri : The Great Escarpment of the Indian Subcontinent*, Vol. II. pp. 919-934. Bangalore: Geological Society of India.

Chamyal L.S. and S.S. Merh. 1995. The Quaternary Formations of Gujarat. In Quaternary Environments and Geoarchaeology of India, Geological Society of India Memoir 32. (Eds. Wadia S., R. Korisettar and V.S. Kale), pp. 246-257. Bangalore: Geological Society of India.

Deo S.G., Savita Ghate, Arati Deshpande-Mukherjee and P.P. Joglekar 2001. Geomorphological Observations at and around Kelshi Region, Konkan Coast, Maharashtra, *Man and Environment* 26(1): 69-74.

Ghate Savita 1985. Late Quaternary Palaegeography of the Littoral zone of the North Konkan, Maharashtra. Unpublished Ph.D. Thesis, University of Pune.

Ghate Savita.1988. Sea Level Fluctuations of North Konkan with Special Reference to Sopara. *Current Science* 57(24): 1317-1320.

Ghate Savita 1990. Palaeogeography of Chaul: A Coastal Town on North Konkan Coast. Bulletin of the Deccan College Post-Graduate & Research Institute 49: 145-151.

Gogte Vishwas D. 2003. Discovery of the Ancient Port of Chaul. Man and Environment XXVIII (1): 67-74.

Gupta Anil.K. D.M. Anderson and J.T. Overpack. 2003. Abrupt changes in the Asian Southwest Monsoon during the Holocene and their links to the North Atlantic Ocean. Nature 421(23): 354-357.

Gupta S.P., Sunil Gupta, Tejas Garge, Rohini Pandey, Anuja Geetali and Sonali Gupta. 2004. On the Fast Track of the Periplus: Excavations at Kamrej –2003. Jounra of Indian Ocean Archaeology (1): 9-33.

Guzder S. 1980. *Quternary Environments and Stone Age Cultures of the Konkan Coast, Maharashtra, India.* Pune : Deccan College.

Joshi R.V. and B.P. Bopardikar. 1972. Stone Age Cultures of Konkan (Coastal Maharashtra), in S.B. Deo Ed. Archaeological Congress and Seminar Papers, pp. 42-52. Nagpur: Nagpur University.

Joglekar P.P., S.G. Deo, Arati Deshpande-Mukherjee and Savita Ghate 2001-2002. Archaeological Investigation at Kelshi, District Ratnagiri, Maharashtra, *Puratattva* 32: 63-73, 224.

Malik S. 1963. Studies in the Prehistory of Western India with special Reference to Gujarat. Ph.D. Dissertation. Pune: University of Pune.

Marathe A.R. 2004. Acheulian Cave at Susrondi, Konkan, Maharashtra. *Current Science* 90: 1538-1544.

Mathur U.B. 2005. *Quaternary Geology: Indian Perspective.* Memoir 63 Geological Society of India: Bangalore.

Rajaguru S.N. and Sushama G. Deo. 2005. Coastal Geomorphology of Sanjan: A Preliminary Report. *Journal of Indian Ocean Archaeology* (2): 93-98, Plate X.

Sankalia, H.D.1962. Stone Age Cultures of Bombay: A Re-appraisal. *Journal of Asiatic Society, Bombay* (34-35): 120-131.

Sharma Sukanya 2001.Cultural Affinities between Southeast Asia and Northeast India during Prehistoric times with special reference to Ganol and Rongraam Valleys in Meghalyala. Unpublished Ph.D. Dissertation, Pune: University of Poona.

Thokchom Angou S.1987. Quaternary Studies in the Manipur Valley. Unpublished Ph.D. Dissertation, Pune: University of Poona.

Todd, K.R.U. 1939. Palaeolithic Industries of Bombay. *Journal of the Royal Anthropological Institute* LXIX: 257-272.

FAUNAL REMAINS FROM SANJAN, DISTRICT VALSAD, GUJARAT

P.P. Joglekar

Deccan College
Pune 411 006

Introduction

Gupta *et al* (2002-2003) conducted excavations at the ancient site of Sanjan (District Valsad, Gujarat) for two field seasons in the years 2002 and 2003. The excavators have identified that the site to be occupied between the eight and the tenth centuries A.D. This report is based on the faunal material handed over to the author. This report aims to provide a complete picture of the faunal material recovered at Sanjan, the methods of analysis used and documentation of quantitative and metrical data. Therefore, besides discussion of the role played by animals in the subsistence economy of people at Sanjan, primary data of faunal identification are given in both graphical and tabular formats. Since the utility of faunal reports for future comparative analyses is largely dependent on the methods and the sampling frames used, standard archaeozoological methods (Reitz and Wing 1999:371-272) were practiced. Further, a standard protocol of the laboratory analysis, data storage and quantitative analysis developed at the archaeozoological laboratory at Deccan College was followed. The faunal collection from both SJN-K and SJN-B contains a good number of shells of molluscs. These were isolated for more intensive study to be done by a specialist in malaco-archaeozoology and hence are excluded from this report.

ARCHAEOZOOLOGICAL METHODS AND THE TAXA INDENTIFIED

The faunal material collected from both the localities, i.e. Bandar (SJN-B) and Koliwada (SJN-K) was mechanically cleaned and then thoroughly washed. The material was dried in shed to avoid cracks due to sunlight. Wherever necessary, recently broken fragments (during recovery and transporting) were mended. The method prescribed by Clason (1972) for counting the specimens was used, in which ancient fragments of a single skeletal element were not treated as separate entities. In the case of bones showing ancient cut marks, these were counted as separate specimens. After initial cleaning the material was sorted into two broad categories - axial skeletal elements (ribs, vertebrae and skull) and elements of the appendicular skeleton (limbs).

Identification of the skeletal elements up to the species level was carried out with help of standard reference skeletons available at the Deccan College. In case of a few closely related species (e.g. sheep and goat; ox, buffalo and nilgai) either ready-made identification keys (Schmid 1972) or those prepared newly at Deccan College (e.g. Joglekar *et al.* 1994; Pawankar and Thomas 2001) were used. In spite of a careful study of species distinguishing markers or the morphological features a few elements could not be assigned to a particular specie or genus. This was the case with fragmentary ribs, vertebrae, carpals and tarsals, phalanges and a number of cranial bones. Such fragments were grouped into broad classes such as *Bos/Bubalus* (cattle or buffalo), *Capra/Ovis* (goat or sheep) and `small ruminant'. The class of `small ruminant' includes goat, sheep, blackbuck, chinkara (four-horned antelope) and gazelle. A few of bird bones found in the collection were identified using criteria prepared for distinguishing among different bird families (Joglekar 1990).

The results of bone identification and bone measurements (von den Driesch 1976) were recorded in the computerized coded format used at the Deccan College. Each bone fragment was thoroughly examined to find out the impact of both pre- and post-depositional factors. Bone modification includes intentional fractures (Sadek-Kooros 1975) as well as accidental breakage of bones both in the past and after their recovery during the excavation process. Author's unpublished observations carried out on carnivores such as hyena, jackals, dogs and cats were used for understanding the bone modification done by these carnivores. DCPARZ –computer software developed at the archaeozoology laboratory by the author in late 1980s was used to analyse the bones recoded in the prescribed format. Bones collected from the pits and dumps are discussed separately. Since the computerized analysis procedure requires these units to be treated distinctly, these archaeological features are given separate code numbers.

SJN-K: NATURE OF THE FAUNAL MATERIAL

The entire collection of animal remains done from SJN-K mound was examined. The fragments collected from archaeological features such as pits and structures were treated separately. These include four pits sealed by layer 1 and a platform of the same layer. The faunal material from SJN-K consisted small to large fragments.

Out of total 1642 fragments 753 (45.86%) could be identified (NISP). It was not possible to identify remaining 889 fragments (Table 2 and Fig. 1). These unidentified

Table 1 Animal taxa identified at Sanjan (B and K localities)

Domestic mammals	Other mammals	Non-mammalian taxa
Bos indicus (cattle)	*Bos gaurus* (gaur)	*Gallus domesticus* (fowl)
Bubalus bubalis (buffalo)	*Bubalus arnee* (wild buffalo)	*Pavo cristatus* (peafowl)
Capra hircus (goat)	*Boselaphus tragocamelus* (nilgai)	*Kachuga tecta* (Indian Sawback turtle)
Ovis aries (sheep)	*Axis axis* (chital)	*Lissemys punctata* (Indian Flapshell turtle)
Sus domesticus (pig)	*Cervus unicolor (*sambar)	Marine Fish (very small)
Canis familiaris (dog)	*Tetracerus quadricornis* (chinkara)	Marine Fish (small)
Equus caballus (horse)	*Antilope cervicapra* (blackbuck)	Marine Fish (medium)
Equus asinus (ass)	*Gazella bennetti* (gazelle)	Marine Fish (Large)
	Canis lupus (wolf)	*Wallago atta*
	Herpestes edwardsii (mongoose)	Marine Crab
	Funambulus sp. (squirrel)	
	Rattus rattus (house rat)	
	Bandicota indica (bandicoot rat)	
	Lepus nigricollis (hare)	

Table 2 Sanjan-K: Summary of animal bone identification

Layer/Unit coding	Description of archaeological feature	NISP	UF	TF	%NISP
1	Layer 1	433	526	959	45.15
2	Layer 2	174	155	329	52.89
3	Layer 3	84	161	245	34.29
4	Layer 4	13	7	20	-
*17	Above HS1 (A4 NW-B4 NE) Sec. Pit	6	0	6	-
*18	Pit in B4 sealing layer 1	8	0	8	-
*19	Pit in B5 sealing layer 1	4	0	4	-
*20	Pit in B5 sealing layer 1	18	0	18	-
*21	Pit M in B5 sealing layer 1	11	20	31	-
*22	Platform (A3 SW: 0.24-0.36 m) layer 1	1	20	21	-
*23	Brushing (A4 SW: 0.53 m) layer 2	1	0	1	-
Total		753	889	1642	45.86

fragments (UF) were divided into three categories (Table 3 and Fig.2): small (<2 cm), medium (2-5 cm) and large (>5 cm). It is clear from the distribution that majority of fragments in all the three layers were small in size. It has been observed that several identified fragments and a large number of unidentified fragments had rolled edges. The condition of the unidentified fragments indicates that the animal bones after their deposition have undergone some physical movement or were crushed/trampled. This is particularly true in case of layer 3 at SJN-K where almost all small-sized unidentified fragments show marks of post-depositional physical damage/movement within the deposit. Similarly, a few fragments from layer 2 bear signatures of post-depositional modifications. For instance, a fragment of horizontal ramus of ox mandible and distal end of ox tibia had cracked surfaces. Also a few bones collected from layer 1 such as humerus bones of cattle, buffalo, blackbuck and deer bear marks of prolonged weathering. Surfaces of these bones show criss-cross cracking pattern, perhaps indicating that these fragments were exposed to sunlight for a considerable time before getting buried in the soil.

A few cases of bones found together in their correct anatomical sequence tell us about the manner of butchering/carcass processing and discarding the unwanted portions like carpals, tarsals and phalanges. From trench A3-SE (layer 1) at 0.30 m level, three cattle phalanges (SJN027, 028 and 029) were found. All these belong to a single adult. However, in general it seems that most of the discarded skeletal elements/ units in all three layers have not been found in their primary depositional context. The fragments found in all the four layers were classified into three types depending on their meat content: A (High Meat), B (Medium Meat) and C (No Meat) using the system proposed by Uerpmann (1973). The distribution of these three types of fragments in SJN-K (Fig. 3-4) shows that non-meat bearing parts are less represented in the collection than their expected proportion based on their numbers in animal body.

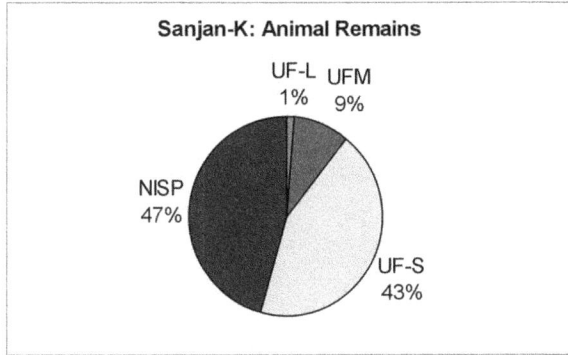

Fig. 1

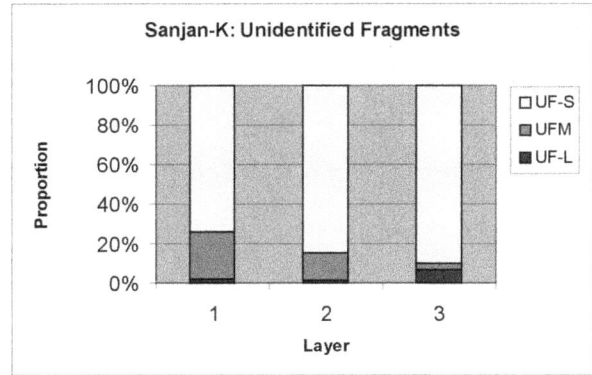

Fig. 2

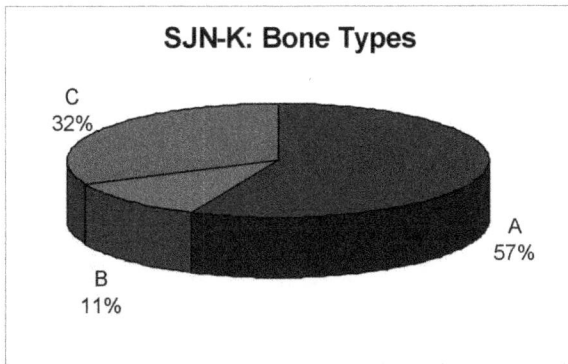

Fig. 3

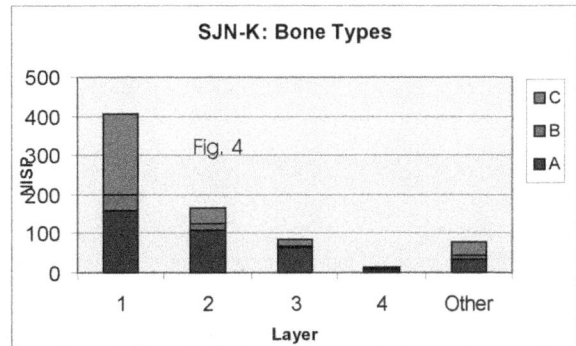

Fig. 4

Table 3 Sanjan-K: Unidentified fragments and their weight

Layer/Unit	UF-large	UF-medium	UF-Small	UF
1	9 (39)	128 (232)	389 (404)	526 (675)
2	2 (10)	21 (46)	127 (164)	150 (220)
3	11 (44)	5 (13)	145 (161)	161 (218)
4	0	0	7 (8)	7 (8)
Other Units	0	0	45 (48)	48 (54)
Total	*22 (93)*	*154 (291)*	*713 (785)*	*889 (1169)*

Figures in parentheses are of weight (g)

In most of the cases ancient breaks occurred when the fragments were in fresh condition. In some cases the broken/cut pieces of the bone were found together. For example, a distal end of buffalo metacarpal was broken into six pieces that were found together in trench A4 (SW) from layer 1 at 0.50 m level. The observation A good number of bones bear cut marks while charring marks were seen on less 5% bones (Table 4). In case of 10 fragments marks of butchering/carcass processing were visible (Plate I: A and B).

Marks of modifications done by carnivores (possibly dogs) were visible on two fragments recovered from layer 1 at SJN-K: a first phalanx of cattle (Trench A4, SW quadrant) and sheep/goat mandible (Trench A3, SE quadrant). Three bone fragments found from layer 1 indicated that these were gnawed either by rodents like house rats or bandicoots. These include one cattle second phalanx, a horn core of blackbuck and a metatarsal bone of nilgai.

It is a common observation that rats and bandicoots inhabit the archaeological sites of historical as well as medieval periods. It is possible to identify the bones of these animals as later date intrusions within the archaeological sites or of animals contemporary to the archaeological habitation. At SJN-K only one such later intrusion was seen in layer 1 (within a pit Trench B5). Layer 1 assemblage showed presence of four other rat bones. However, the condition of these bones indicates that these rats were living at the time of ancient habitation at Sanjan. It is interesting to note that the faunal collection contained a number of bone tools (Plate I: C) and some fragments indicating bone

Table 4 Sanjan-K: Bone modifications

Layer	(1)	(2)	(3)	(4)	Other units	Total	%*
Charred	04	04	01	00	00	09	1.19
Charred completely	03	05	04	00	01	13	1.73
Charred and calcified	04	01	02	00	00	07	0.93
Cut marks	29	18	19	02	00	68	9.03
Gnawing marks	03	00	00	00	00	03	0.40
Butchering marks	04	01	03	00	02	10	1.33
Carnivore teeth marks	02	00	00	00	00	02	0.26
Later intrusions	00	00	00	00	01	01	0.13
Tools/attempted tools	04	01	01	01	00	07	0.93

* With respect to total NISP= 753

A

B

C

PLATE I

D

modification in an attempt to make tools or objects (Plate I: D). At SJN-K there are 7 such tools of which 4 are from layer 1 (Table 4).

SJN-B: NATURE OF THE FAUNAL MATERIAL

The entire faunal collection done from Koliwada site (SJN-K) in 2003 was examined. However, owing to the large quantity of bones recovered from the Bandar site (SJN-B), a sampling strategy was adopted. At SJN-B, layers 5 to 7 have yielded not more than 200 fragments (Table 5). Hence, all material from these layers was studied. The material collected from layers 1 to 4 at SJN-B was in small paper packets. These packets were counted and a quarter of the packets were chosen at random for further examination. Thus this report of faunal remains from SJN-B is based on a random sample of representative material from layers 1 to 4.

Table 5 Sanjan-B: Summary of animal bone identification

Layer	NISP	UF	TF	% NISP
1#	219	187	406	53.94
2#	281	236	517	54.35
3#	277	153	430	64.42
4#	343	139	482	71.16
5	67	49	116	57.76
6	53	21	74	71.62
7	22	4	26	84.61
Total	**1262**	**789**	**2051**	**61.53**

25% sample examined

Out of total 2051 fragments number of identified specimens (NISP) were 1262 (61.53%). As compared to SJN-K more fragments could be identified (Fig. 5). This was because here in general, the faunal material is better preserved. A total of 789 fragments could not be identified and the level of identification was between 54-85 % (Fig. 6). It was not possible to identify remaining 889 fragments. These unidentified fragments (UF) were divided into three categories in the same way as has been done in case of SJN-K (Table 6 and Fig. 7): small (<2 cm), medium (2-5 cm) and large (>5 cm). It is clear from the distribution of these fragments that the proportion of large and medium fragments is more than that of small fragments. The pattern of ancient breaks and cut marks seen on both identified

and unidentified fragments indicates that here the faunal material was subjected to lesser degree of physical damage, crushing and other such post-depositional changes. Like SJN-K the faunal material from SJN-B also consisted small to large fragments. However, the condition of the bones from SJN-B was remarkably different than those found at SJN-K. In this mound fragments found from a few lots were porous in nature. For example, almost all fragments collected from trench TT1 (quadrant SW) at 0.95 m level (layer 3) were porous and light in weight. Almost entire collection from trench TT1 (quadrant SE, 0.72 m level, layer 2) was in a similar condition. These were perhaps in the areas of water logging. Also in case of a good number of fragments the edges were rolled and adraded. Some of these were so rounded that these looked like balls of amorphous nature

The classification of fragments into the types based on meat value (Fig. 8-9) revealed that like SJN-K here too the fragments that have no meat value are less than their expected value. If the animals are butchered and carcasses are processed within the settlement, bones of no meat value such as tarsals, carpals and phalanges are expected within the deposit. However, the observed distribution shows that both at SJN-B and SJN-K animals were mostly butchered and mostly the meat-bearing parts were brought within the habitation area and the bones were deposited after consumption.

The proportion of later date intrusions in SJN-B is more

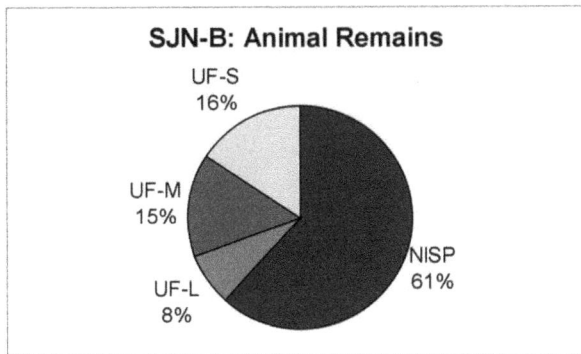
Fig. 5

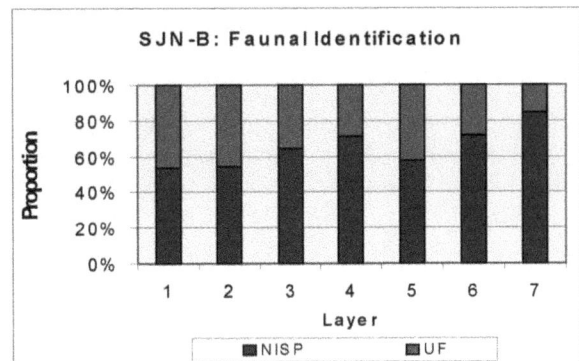
Fig. 6

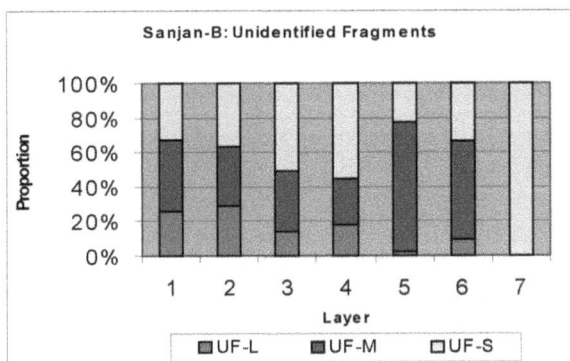
Fig. 7

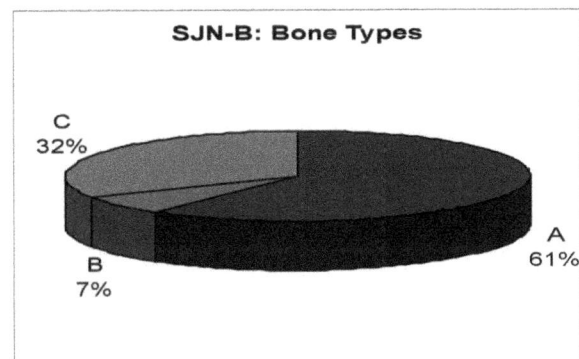
Fig. 8

Table 6 Sanjan-B: Unidentified fragments and their weight

Layer	UF-large	UF-medium	UF-Small	UF
1	48 (294)	78 (176)	61 (73)	187 (543)
2	68 (290)	81 (146)	87 (96)	236 (532)
3	21 (98)	54 (100)	78 (85)	153 (283)
4	25 (102)	37 (86)	77 (81)	139 (269)
5	1 (8)	37 (74)	11 (14)	49 (96)
6	2(10)	12 (22)	7 (10)	21 (42)
7	0	0	4 (6)	4 (6)
Total	**165 (802)**	**299 (604)**	**325 (365)**	**789 (1771)**

Figures in parentheses are of weight (g)

Table 7 Sanjan-B: Bone modifications

Layer	1	2	3	4	5	6	7	Total	%*
Charred	1	1	2	1	2	2	1	10	0.79
Charred completely	1	1	1	2	2	0	0	7	0.55
Charred and calcified	1	0	0	1	0	0	0	2	0.16
Cut marks	8	11	12	14	4	15	8	72	5.71
Gnawing marks	1	0	1	2	2	0	0	6	0.48
Butchering marks	2	2	1	2	1	1	0	9	0.71
Carnivore teeth marks	0	0	1	1	1	0	0	3	0.24
Later intrusions	0	2	1	16	4	0	0	23	1.82
Tools/attempted tools	0	1	0	0	0	1	1	3	0.24
Object/Ornament	0	0	0	0	1	0	0	1	0.08

* With respect to total NISP= 1262

than that seen at SJN-K that includes both house rats and bandicoots (Table 7). It is necessary to note that 16 bones of bandicoots were found in layer 4 (TT1, NW, 1.61 m). The condition of these bones is different than other layer 4 bones and clearly these represent later date (any time between the deposition of layer 4 and now) intruding activity in the archaeological deposit. These include ribs, mandibles, pelvic bones and long bones. However, one femur found from trench TT1 (SE) of layer 2 at 1.05 m level is clearly not a later intrusion. This animal perhaps lived contemporary to the habitation/deposition of layer 2. This bone does not have any marks of cutting or charring and hence was not part of the diet of the inhabitants. All rat skeletal elements found from SJN-B are later date intrusions in the habitation

As compared to SJN-K, the proportion of animal bones showing charring activity is less. Only 1.5% of the fragments were charred, completely burnt or were calcified due to long exposure to intense heat. Same observation is made about cut marks and marks left by blades while butchering/carcass processing. In SJN-K about 9% fragments showed such marks, while only 6% fragments from SJN-B bear marks of butchering (Plate V: A) and

carcass processing (Table 7). A case of humerus of a male spotted deer (SJN221) is interesting. The blade has made a sharp cut, but it has gone only halfway though the bone cortex. Only three bone tools have been found at SJN-B (Plate V: B).

Two fragments showed marks of modifications done by carnivores. These include a goat calacaneum bone from layer 1 (trench TT2-SE, depth 1.24 m) and another goat radius from layer 5 (Trench TT2, SE, depth 2.46 m). Both marks were due to gnawing and chewing by canids like dogs. Marks of gnawing done by rodents were seen in case of six fragments. These include a humerus fragment of blackbuck from layer 5, a calacaneum of blackbuck from layer 4, the pelvic bone of sheep from layer 4.and an astragalus of cattle found from layer 1.

A few lots from SJN-B give some clues to understanding the utilization and bone deposition pattern. For example, in trench TT1 (SW, layer 7) at 3.76 m level two fragments of sheep scapula were found. These fragments (SJN201, 204) belonged to left side of an adult that was cut, consumed and discarded together. Similarly, a fragment of humerus and ulna were found in trench TT1 (SW, layer 7) at 3.35 m level.

A

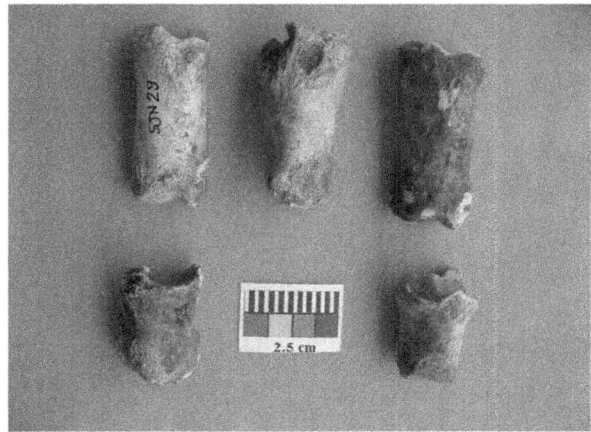

B

C

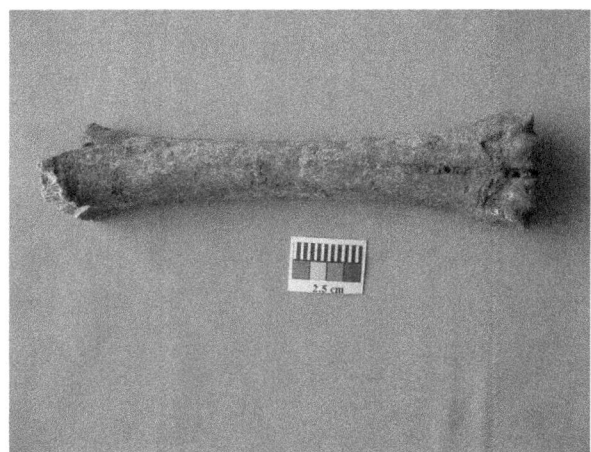

D

PLATE II

Both were of the right side of the body ((SJN212, 215) and belonged to an adult male blackbuck. Also a fragment of femur of another animal, an adult doe of the same species was found in the same trench. However, other body parts of these have not been deposited in the same context. It is likely that only limb parts of these animals were brought back to the settlement and consumed.

SJN-K

Domestic Mammals at SJN-K

The proportion of domestic mammals at SJN-K is as large as 71% (537/753) and the species include cattle, buffalo, goat, pig, horse and ass (Table 8-9, Fig. 10). It is clear from the pattern of cut marks and butchering marks that the horse, ass and dog were not used as food.

The cattle and buffalo formed the major part of the assemblage at SJN-K in which the later species was consumed to a lesser degree (Plate II: A-B). The cattle age-sex distribution seen in all the layers in general shows that both young and old cattle of both sexes were culled and consumed. In the baulk material from layer 1, fourteen bones of a single animal were found together. These include pre-maxilla, partial cranium, metatarsal, 4 first phalanges,

3 second phalanges and one third phalanx. The condition of the bones and absence of any marks of butchering/charring shows that this individual was a young animal (sex indeterminate) of age less than 2 years, and that it was buried. The occurrence of bones of hind leg in the serial order (as they are in the body) reveals that this burial was not disturbed. It seems that only two parts of this individual: skull and hind leg were selectively kept, purpose of which is not possible to know from the faunal record.

A total of 17 skeletal elements could be identified definitely as of buffalo of which 6 came from a pit above HS1 in trenches A4 NW-B4 NE (unit *17). The skeletal elements found in this pit include remains of a single animal: maxilla, metacarpal, magnum, first phalanx and two second phalanges. This was a small-sized buffalo (perhaps a female) and all these bones are devoid of any marks. It is likely that this female was not culled for food and was simply buried in the pit. The other skeletal elements of the buffalo include cranial and post-cranial elements of which two bear marks of charring and butchering. It is interesting that a distal end of humerus found in layer 1 (trench A3-NW at 0.37 m level) was used as a tool. From the tooth wearing pattern and epiphyseal fusion it is clear that both young and old individuals were culled at SJN-K. Both sheep and goat were used for food at SJN-K and together they formed

17

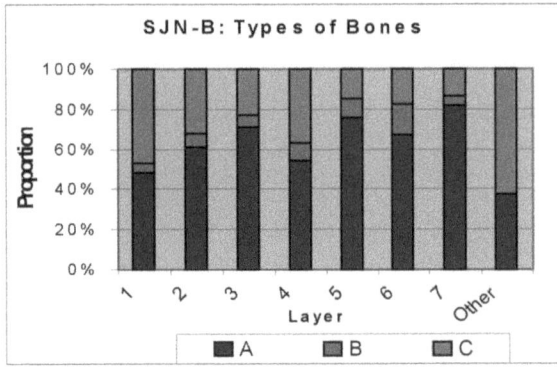

Fig. 9

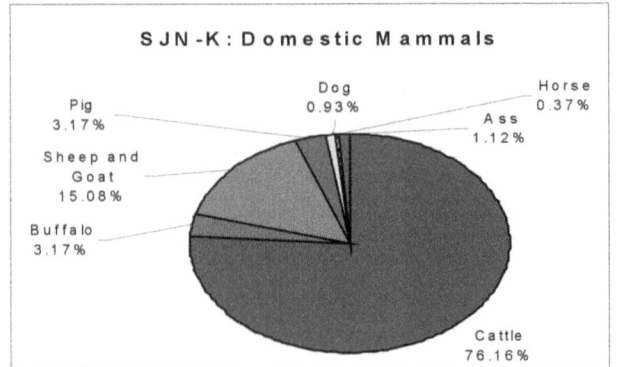

Fig. 10

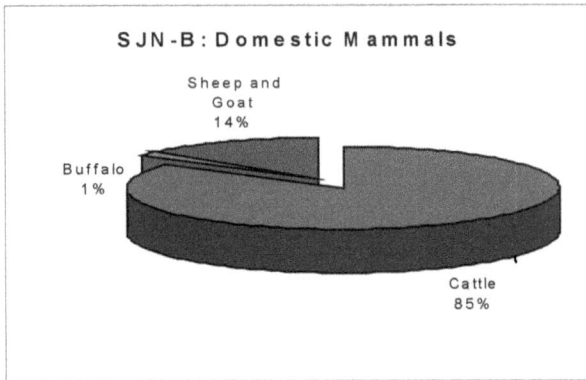

Fig. 11

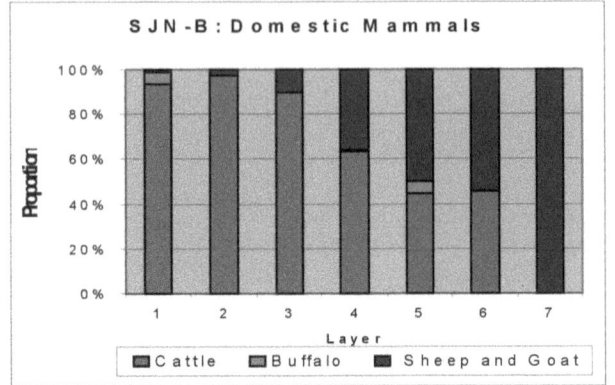

Fig. 12

A

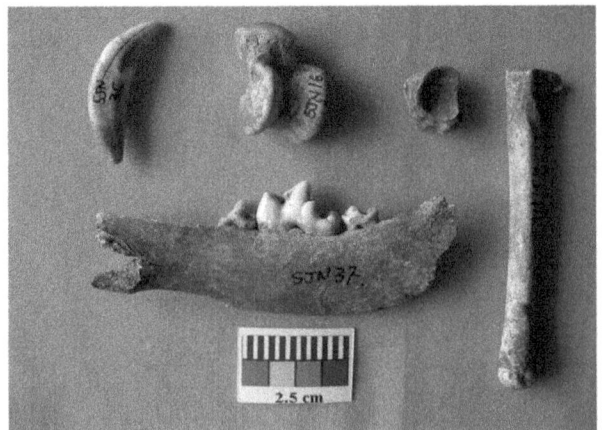

B

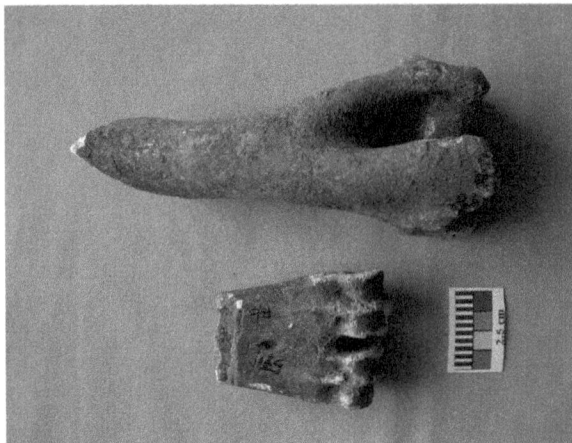

C

PLATE III

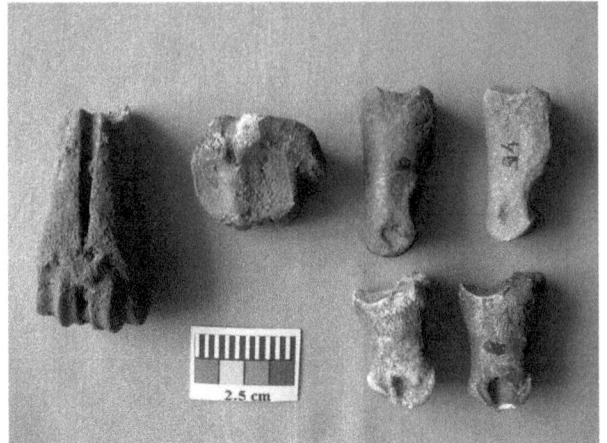

D

Table 8 Sanjan-K: Animal remains (NISP) from other archaeological features

Species/Taxonomic Unit	*17	*18	*19	*20	*21	*22	*23	Total	Weight
Bos indicus	0	0	1	0	3	0	0	4	40
Bos/Bubalus	0	5	0	2	4	0	0	11	58
Bubalus bubalis	6	0	0	0	0	0	0	6	272
Capra hircus (domestic)	0	0	0	1	1	0	0	2	10
Boselaphus tragocamelus	0	1	0	0	0	0	0	1	80
Axis axis	0	0	0	1	0	0	1	2	22
Small Ruminant	0	2	2	10	0	1	0	15	34
Sus domesticus	0	0	0	2	2	0	0	4	13
Rattus rattus	0	0	1	0	0	0	0	1	1
Small mammal-hare size	0	0	0	1	0	0	0	1	1
Gallus domesticus	0	0	0	1	0	0	0	1	1
Kachuga tecta	0	0	0	0	1	0	0	1	1
Total	**6**	**8**	**4**	**18**	**11**	**1**	**1**	**49**	**533**

Table 9 Sanjan-K: Animal species identified (NISP) from layer 1 to 4

Layer	1		2		3		4
Species/Taxonomic Unit	NISP	%NISP	NISP	%NISP	NISP	%NISP	NISP
Bos indicus	69	15.94	8	4.60	2	2.38	0
Bos/Bubalus	213	49.19	73	41.95	29	34.52	0
Bubalus bubalis	6	1.39	3	1.72	2	2.38	0
Capra hircus (domestic)	6	1.39	3	1.72	1	1.19	0
Capra hircus/Ovis aries	23	5.31	36	20.69	6	7.14	0
Ovis aries	0	0.00	3	1.72	1	1.19	0
Sus domesticus	11	2.54	2	1.15	0	0	0
Canis familiaris	5	1.15	0	0.00	0	0	0
Equus caballus	1	0.23	0	0.00	1	1.19	0
Equus asinus	6	1.39	0	0.00	0	0	0
Gallus domesticus	1	0.23	0	0.00	0	0	0
Boselaphus tragocamelus	4	0.92	0	0.00	0	0	0
Axis axis	16	3.70	7	4.02	4	4.76	0
Cervus unicolor	2	0.46	0	0.00	0	0	0
Tetracerus quadricornis	3	0.69	0	0.00	0	0	1
Antilope cervicapra	8	1.85	2	1.15	0	0	0
Lepus nigricollis	6	1.39	2	1.15	0	0	1
Small mammal-hare size	1	0.23	1	0.57	0	0	1
Rattus rattus	4	0.92	0	0.00	0	0	0
Small Ruminant	32	7.39	21	12.07	35	41.67	9
Herpestes edwardsii	0	0.00	1	0.57	0	0	0
Funambulus sp.	0	0.00	0	0.00	1	1.19	0
General Bird Bone	3	0.69	0	0.00	0	0	0
General Reptile Bone	0	0.00	0	0.00	1	1.19	0
Kachuga tecta	1	0.23	0	0.00	0	0	0
Marine fish unidentified	0	0.00	1	0.57	0	0	0
Marine Fish (very small)	0	0.00	1	0.57	0	0	0

Layer	1		2		3		4
Marine Fish (small)	3	0.69	4	2.30	0	0	1
Marine Fish (medium)	7	1.62	4	2.30	1	1.19	0
Marine Fish (Large)	1	0.23	0	0.00	0	0	0
Wallago atta	1	0.23	2	1.15	0	0	0
Total	**433**	**100**	**174**	**100**	**84**	**100**	**13**

A

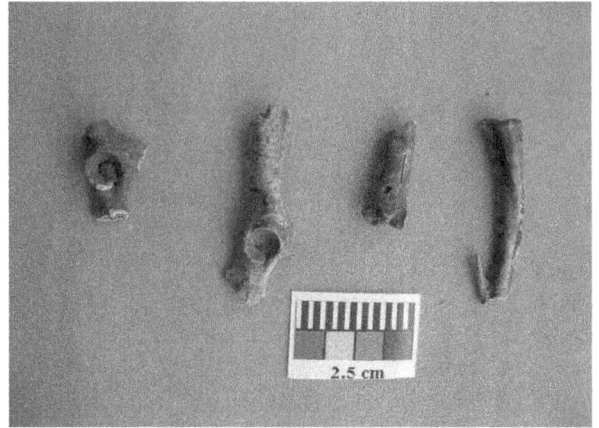

B

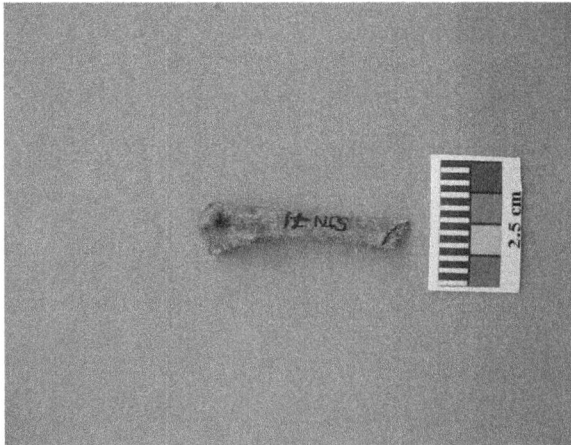

C

PLATE IV

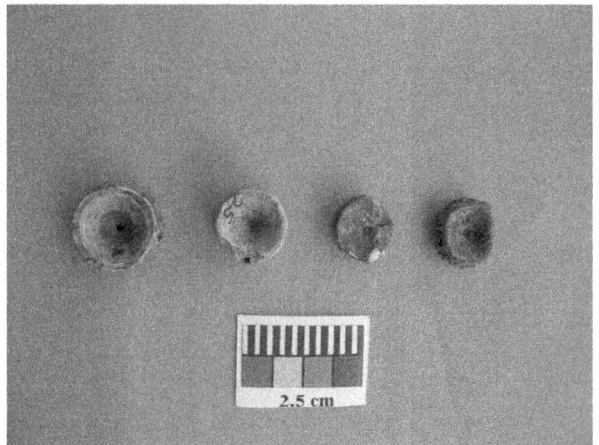

D

about 15% of the total domestic mammalian remains. It was possible to identify 12 skeletal elements as of goat and 4 of sheep, respectively. Several of the bones of sheep and goat bear cut and charring marks. From the wear pattern of the teeth it can be concluded that most of these animals were culled at an early age. This indicates that perhaps these animals were more valued for their meat than other products.

A total of 17 skeletal elements of the domestic pig bones were found from layer 1,2 and other archaeological features (Table 10, Plate III: A). Most of the skeletal elements belonged to the skull/head category and only isolated fragments of the fore foot and foot portions were found. It is interesting that most of the pigs were young when

Table10 Sanjan-K: Distribution of skeletal elements of domestic pig

Skeletal Type\Layer	1	2	*20	*21	Total
Head	11	2	0	1	14
Axial	0	0	0	0	0
Forequarter	0	0	0	0	0
Hindquarter	0	0	0	0	0
Fore foot	0	0	1	1	2
Hind foot	0	0	0	0	0
Foot	0	0	1	0	1

cut and consumed. This indicates that the pig was perhaps not reared on a large-scale at SJN-K and perhaps pork was brought into the settlement from outside.

The evidence of horse at SJN-K (Plate IV: A) is in the form of two skeletal elements: an upper molar found from trench A4-NE (layer 1) and a fragment of occipital bone found from trench B3-NE (layer 3). Both these elements are devoid of any marks. Thus it can be concluded that this beast of burden was not consumed. Similarly, the ass was not consumed at SJN-K. The evidence of ass is from a single lot from trench A5-SW layer 1 at 0.33 m level, where 6 maxillary teeth of a single animal (three molars and three molars) were found. Only five dog bones were found at SJN-K in layer 1: a mandible, isolated lower canine, metatarsal, astragalus and the tarsal found below astragalus (Plate III: B). All these were found from 0.16 to 0.19 m level in which two individuals (both adults of a same size) could be recognised.

Wild Mammals at SJN-K

The wild mammals utilized as food at SJN-K include three species of antelopes, two deer species, hare, squirrel and a small mammalian species. A few bones of nilgai (*Boselaphus tragocamelus*) were found from SJN-K, that include distal portion of humerus, an ulna bearing a cut mark and distal end of a metacarpal bone of a female (Plate III: C). Two teeth (second maxillary molar and an incisor) were found from layer 1 at 0.20 m level and these belonged to an adult and another very old animal. Only four skeletal elements of four-horned antelope (*Tetracerus quadricornis*) were found, of which three are maxillary molars and an astragalus. The astragalus found from layer 4 (0.83 m level) bears a cut mark on its distal-anterior surface. Only 10 skeletal elements of blackbuck (*Antilope cervicapra*) were found which include fragmented horn cores, mandible, tibia, metacarpal, metatarsal and maxillary molar. One of the molars indicates that it came from a very young animal, perhaps less than a year old, whereas another molar belonged to an adult. The distal end of a radius showed both marks of cutting and removing muscles during carcass processing.

Only two bones of sambar (*Cervus unicolor*) – an astragalus and distal end of metatarsal – were found from layer 1 at Sanjan-K. The astragalus has an oblique cut mark and the metatarsal has marks of butchering/carcass processing. Almost all types of skeletal elements of spotted deer (*Axis axis*) have been found at Sanjan-K in various layers (Plate III: D). Three fragments (scapula, metacarpal and pelvic bone) bear cut marks, of which the metacarpal fragment (SJN005) was charred completely. It has been possible to identify sex of the spotted deer in a majority of the cases. Both males and females are represented almost in equal numbers. In layer 1, there were 6 males and 3 females, while layer 2 and 3 has one female and one male, respectively. One shed antler was found from layer 2 (trench B5-SW at 0.44 m level) and this antler perhaps had remained exposed for a long period before getting incorporated into the deposit.

A single bone fragment of the mongoose (*Herpestes edwardsii*) has been found from layer 2. This was a cut fragment of the pelvic bone (SJN109). Similarly, one fragment of distal end of tibia of the tree squirrel (*Funambulus* sp.) has been found from layer 1. This fragment belonged to an adult and bears a mark of charring. A few bones of hare (*Lepus nigricollis*) have been found both within the layers and other archaeological features (Plate IV: B). These include humerus, radius, pelvic bones, femora and tibia. Besides, these four bones of small mammal of the size of hare or smaller animal than that were found. Due to lack of diagnostic features, it was not possible to identify these further. However, these perhaps include both hare and squirrel.

Non-mammalian Remains at SJN-K

The proportion of non-mammalian remains at SJN-K is less in the total collection. These include birds and reptiles. Bird bones are scanty (5) in the collection, of which two could be identified as of domestic fowl - *Gallus domesticus* (Plate IV: C). One of these (a tibia fragment) has been found from Pit in trench B5 (layer 1), and another has been a fragment of proximal portion of radius found in layer 1. Three bones, all perhaps of a small bird of the size of pigeon were found from layer 1. One of these was either radius or carpo-metacarpus, while other two were fragments of tibia and tarso-metatarsus. Only three skeletal elements of reptiles were found at SJN-K. These include two vertebrae of *Kachuga tecta* (Indian Sawback turtle) and a long bone fragment of an unidentified reptilian species (perhaps a lizard). It has been possible to identify three fragments of a catfish (*Wallago atta*) – a cranial fragment from layer 1, and two external spines of the mandible from layer 2. Several vertebrae of marine fish of various sizes were found from SJN-K (Plate IV: D). Due to lack of distinguishing markers, these were grouped in three categories: small (width <10 mm), medium (width 10-20 mm) and large (width >20 mm). These three types of fish vertebrae were found in different proportion in layers 1 to 4, but were not noticed in the material from pits and other archaeological features at SJN-K.

SJN-B

Domestic Mammals at SJN-B

The proportion of domestic mammals at SJN-B is similar to that found at SJN-K. Here domestic mammals formed 65% (823/1262) of the identified specimens. However, as compared to SJN-K, a limited domestic species were noticed at SJN-B (i.e. cattle, buffalo, sheep and goat). In this faunal collection the pig, horse and ass are absent. In general, like SJN-K, the cattle (Plate V: C) and buffalo formed the major part of the assemblage (Table 11-12, Fig. 11). As a whole, cattle were as large as 85%, while the proportion of buffalo is as small as 1%. The skeletal fragments of buffalo identified at SJN-B include a scapula, two humerus, a femur, five maxillary teeth and three mandibular teeth (Plate V: D).

A

B

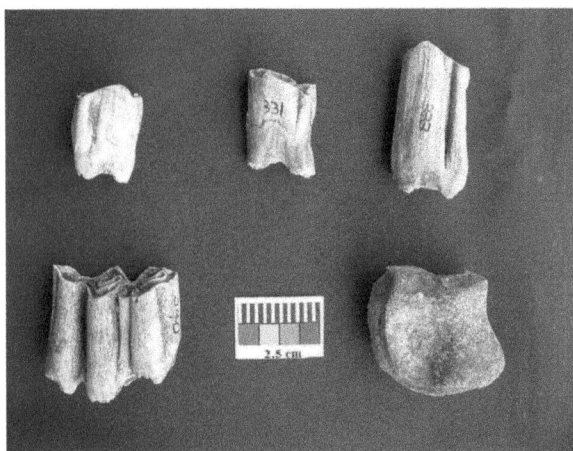

C

PLATE V

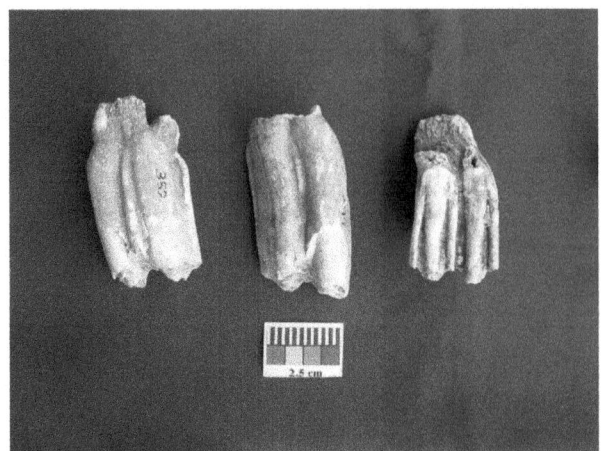

D

The sheep and goat together formed 14% of the faunal assemblage at SJN-B (Plate VI: A-B).. Both sheep and goat were present at SJN-B, where they were used almost to the same degree. The pattern of relative proportion of cattle and buffalo is different in the lower layers (5-7) where sheep and goat were more (Fig. 12). However, it is necessary to note that only a small area of the site has been excavated to this level. Several of the domestic mammalian bones including the buffalo show marks of cutting and charring and hence were valued for their meat.

Wild mammals at SJN-B

The occurrence of bones of wild animals in general indicates that all skeletal elements are not found in the deposit at SJN-B and the frequencies are inadequate for quantitative analysis. Therefore, four wild animal species were grouped as "antelopes" (nilgai, blackbuck, four-horned antelope and gazelle). It has been possible to identify sex of the spotted deer in a few cases: 4 males and 1 female (layer 1), 2 males and 2 females (layer 5), and 1 male and 1 female (layer 7).

From the distribution of skeletal elements of "deer" it is clear that only selected parts of these animals were deposited. If the animals were butchered and consumed within the excavated area, all the skeletal elements are

expected to be deposited. However, fore foot and hind foot that have low meat content are absent. On the other hand elements of high meat utility are found in the deposit. Perhaps this indicates that after discarding less useful parts at the pace of butchery/carcass processing, only the meat-bearing parts of the deer were brought in the settlement and consumed.

All the body parts of the "antelopes" are not found in the settlement. It is likely that these antelopes and gazelles were sporadically hunted/trapped; the high-meat parts were selectively brought into the settlement and their bones discarded after consumption. The four-horned antelope (*Tetracerus quadricornis*) is represented by only their isolated teeth. Of the two teeth found from layer 3 at 3.18 m level, one belonged to an old animal while the other was as young as less than 1 year. The age-sex distribution of the blackbucks (*Antilope cervicapra*) is interesting. Almost all animals (except one each from layer 2 and 3) were adults. Layer 6 shows that two adult males and one adult female were consumed. However, layers 3, 4 and 5 revealed that only females were consumed.

The gazelle bones were found only from layer 2 and 4. In layer 2 only a femur fragment and a completely worn out tooth (upper premolar) of a very old animal were found.

Table 11 Sanjan-B: Identified fragments from layer 1 to 3

Layer	1		2		3	
Species/Taxonomic Unit	NISP	%NISP	NISP	%NISP	NISP	%NISP
Bos indicus	14	7.50	16	5.69	13	4.69
Bos/Bubalus	149	79.70	229	81.49	163	58.84
Bubalus bubalis	9	4.80	0	0.00	0	0.00
Capra hircus (domestic)	0	0.00	0	0.00	9	3.25
Ovis aries	0	0.00	3	1.07	2	0.72
Capra hircus/Ovis aries	2	1.10	4	1.42	9	3.25
Gallus domesticus	0	0.00	2	0.71	1	0.36
Bos gaurus	0	0.00	2	0.71	5	1.81
Bubalus arnee	2	1.10	1	0.36	0	0.00
Boselaphus tragocamelus	0	0.00	0	0.00	0	0.00
Tetracerus quadricornis	0	0.00	0	0.00	2	0.72
Antilope cervicapra	1	0.50	1	0.36	4	1.44
Gazella bennetti	0	0.00	2	0.71	0	0.00
Small Ruminant	6	3.20	13	4.63	62	22.38
Canis lupus	0	0.00	0	0.00	0	0.00
Herpestes edwardsii	0	0.00	0	0.00	1	0.36
Funambulus sp.	0	0.00	0	0.00	0	0.00
Rattus rattus	0	0.00	2	0.71	0	0.00
Bandicota indica	0	0.00	1	0.36	1	0.36
Lepus nigricollis	0	0.00	1	0.36	1	0.36

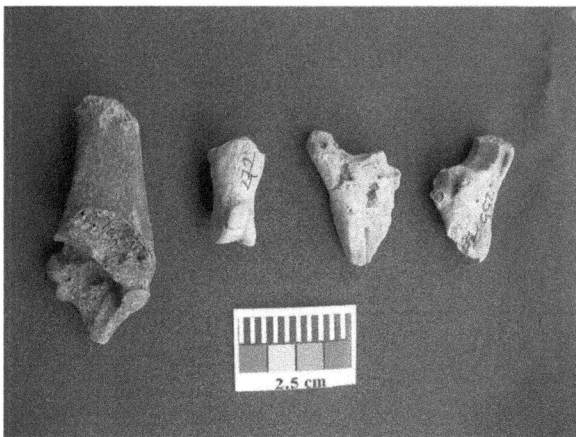

A

B

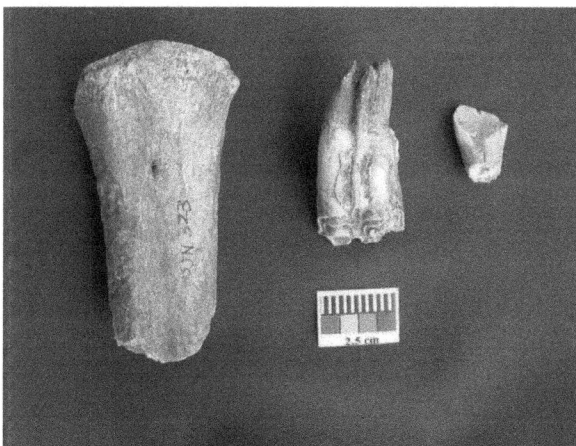

C

PLATE VI

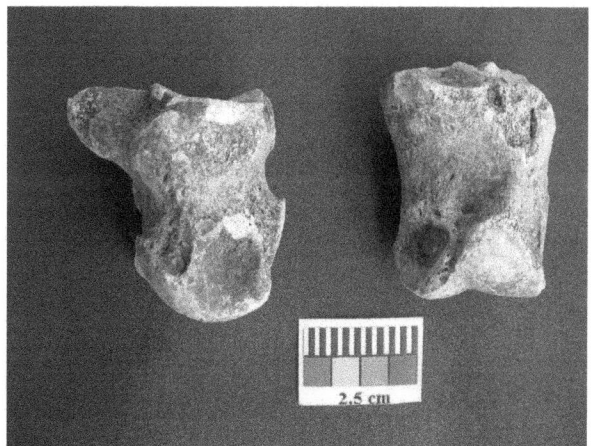

D

23

Layer	1		2		3	
Small mammal-hare size	0	0.00	0	0.00	0	0.00
Pavo cristatus	0	0.00	0	0.00	0	0.00
General Reptile Bone	0	0.00	0	0.00	0	0.00
Lissemys punctata	0	0.00	1	0.36	1	0.36
Fish species unidentified	0	0.00	0	0.00	0	0.00
Marine fish unidentified	1	0.50	0	0.00	0	0.00
Marine Fish (small)	0	0.00	2	0.71	2	0.72
Marine Fish (medium)	3	1.60	1	036	1	0.36
Marine Fish (Large)	0	0.00	0	036	0	0.00
Marine Crab	0	0.00	0	0.00	0	0.00
Total	*187*	*100*	*281*	*100*	*277*	*100*

Table 12 Sanjan-B: Identified fragments from layer 4 to 7

Layer	4		5		6		7
Species/Taxonomic Unit	*NISP*	*%NISP*	*NISP*	*%NISP*	*NISP*	*%NISP*	*NISP*
Bos indicus	8	2.30	0	0.00	0	0.00	0
Bos/Bubalus	95	27.70	8	11.94	5	9.43	0
Bubalus bubalis	1	0.30	1	1.49	0	0.00	0
Capra hircus (domestic)	20	5.80	3	4.48	0	0.00	1
Ovis aries	10	2.90	1	1.49	0	0.00	9
Capra hircus/Ovis aries	28	8.20	5	7.46	6	11.32	0
Gallus domesticus	2	0.60	0	0.00	0	0.00	1
Boselaphus tragocamelus	2	0.60	0	0.00	0	0.00	0
Axis axis	7	2.00	3	4.48	5	9.43	3
Tetracerus quadricornis	1	0.30	0	0.00	0	0.00	0
Antilope cervicapra	14	4.10	4	5.97	8	15.09	2
Gazella bennetti	6	1.70	0	0.00	0	0.00	0
Small Ruminant	114	33.20	33	49.25	18	33.96	2
Canis lupus	0	0.00	0	0.00	1	1.89	0
Lepus nigricollis	0	0.00	0	0.00	1	1.89	0
Funambulus sp.	1	0.30	0	0.00	0	0.00	0
Rattus rattus	1	0.30	4	5.97	0	0.00	0
Bandicota indica	15	4.40	0	0.00	0	0.00	0
Small mammal-hare size	2	0.60	0	0.00	1	1.89	0
Pavo cristatus	1	0.30	0	0.00	0	0.00	0
General Reptile Bone	0	0.00	0	0.00	1	1.89	0
Lissemys punctata	2	0.60	0	0.00	0	0.00	0
Fish species unidentified	0	0.00	0	0.00	1	1.89	0
Marine Fish (small)	4	1.20	1	1.49	2	3.77	0
Marine Fish (medium)	8	2.30	3	4.48	3	5.66	0
Marine Fish (Large)	0	0.00	1	1.49	1	1.89	2
Marine Crab	1	0.30	0	0.00	0	0.00	0
Total	*343*	*100*	*67*	*100*	*53*	*100.00*	*22*

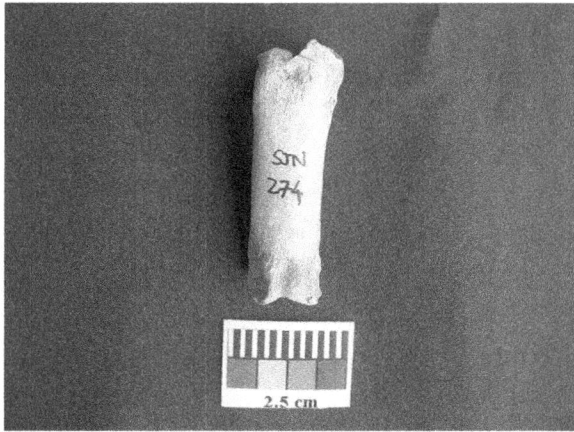

A

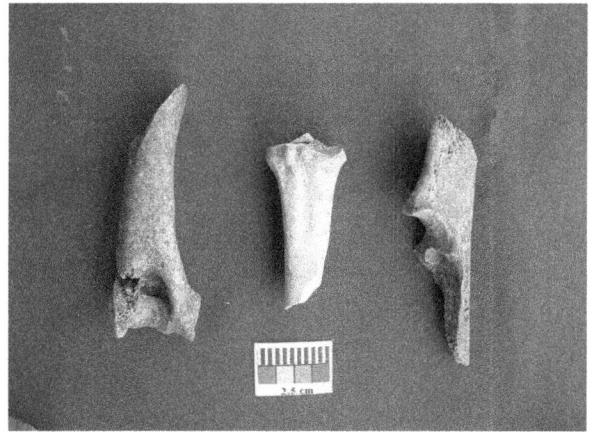

B

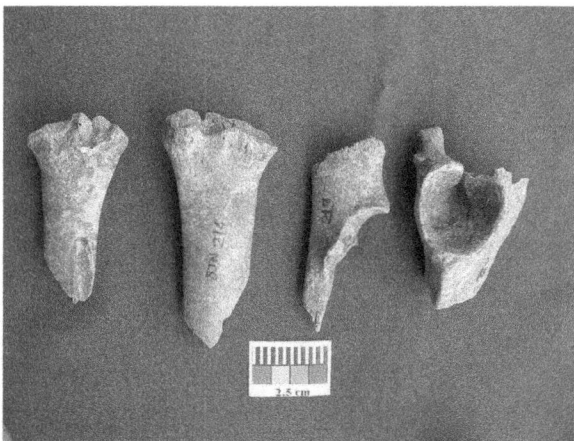

C

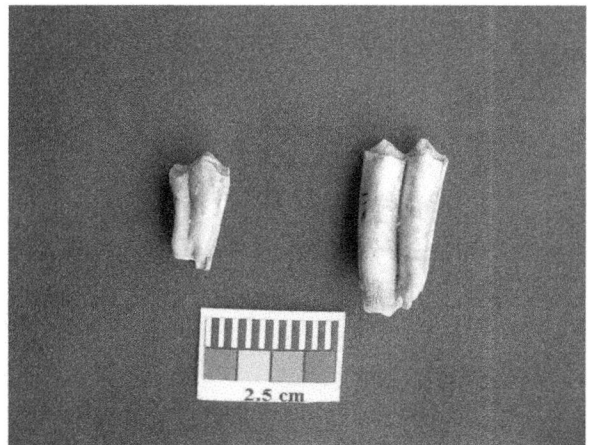

D

PLATE VII

In layer 4 besides the isolated teeth, a second phalanx and charred fragment of pelvic bone were found. In this case also like the four-horned antelope, perhaps a few body parts of these animals had occasionally been brought in the settlement and consumed.

A few isolated bone fragments of two large wild bovids – wild buffalo (*Bubalus arnee*) and gaur (*Bos gaurus*) are found at SJN-B (Plate VI: C-D). There are only three fragments of wild buffalo: a recently damaged first phalanx from layer 1, a second phalanx (SJN344) from layer 1 and another second phalanx (SJN320) from layer 2. There are seven fragments of gaur that include three calcaneum fragments (one with a cut mark), two incisors, one upper second molar and one metatarsal. Out of the three calcaneum fragments found from layer 3 at 0.81 m level is of young animal since the tuber calcis was just fused before the animal's death. Except this case all other skeletal elements belonged to old animals. The metatarsal fragment of the proximal side found from layer 2 at 0.72 m level (SJN323) bears a mark of butchering/ carcass processing.

Three species of wild mammals were represented by a single fragment each: cut portion of a mongoose (*Herpestes edwardsii*) pelvis from layer 3, a tibia fragment of a squirrel (*Funambulus* sp.) from layer 4, and a pelvic bone of a wolf

(*Canis lupus*) from layer 6. All these species perhaps were utilized occasionally. Like SJN-K, the deposit from SJN-B has revealed presence of hare (*Lepus nigricollis*). Three skeletal elements of this species were found: a metacarpal fragment from layer 2, a completely charred tibia fragment from layer 3, and an ulna fragment from layer 6. Besides these a few fragments of some small mammal species were noticed. Like SJN-K, these perhaps include both hare and squirrel or some small species of similar size

Non-mammalian Remains at SJN-B

Like SJN-K the proportion of the non-mammalian remains from SJN-B is small as compared to the mammalian remains. These include birds, reptiles, marine fish of various types and a marine crab species. The skeletal elements of the domestic fowl (*Gallus domesticus*) are humerus, radius, coracoid, carpo-metacarpus and first phalanges. A single fragment of the peafowl () has been found from layer 4 (SJN241) and that this animal was young. As has been *Pavo cristatus* noticed at SJN-K, reptile bones are very few at SJN-B. These include a cranial fragment of a small-sized reptile (lizard/snake) and carapce fragments of the Indian flapshell turtle (*Lissemys punctata*). In this collection, skeletal elements of the Indian sawback turtle (*Kachuga tecta*) are absent. The fish remains from SJN-B are similar

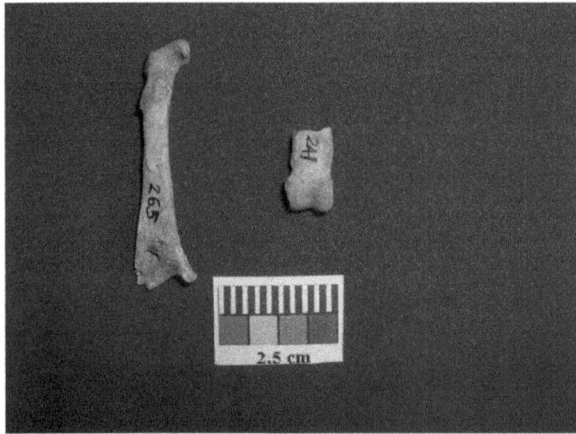

A

B

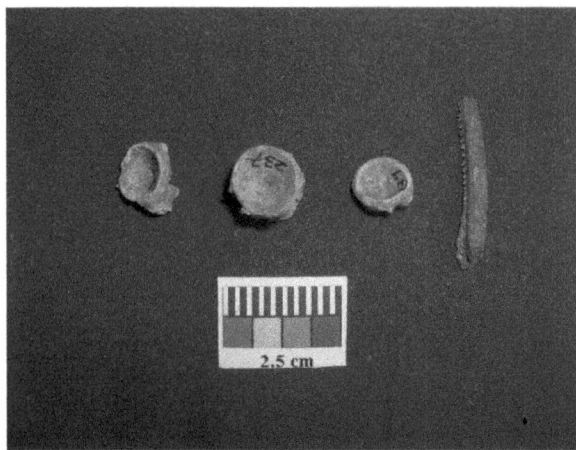

C

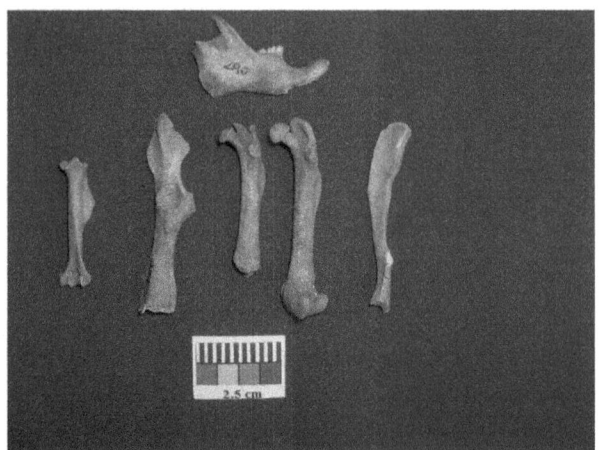

D

PLATE VIII

to those found at SJN-K that include mostly vertebrae and a few cranial fragments of small to large marine fish. The remains could not be identified to any specific species. A single fragment of a chelated leg of a marine crab species (medium size) was found from layer 4 (SJN248). This indicates that besides other marine resources such as molluscs and fish the crabs were also utilized for food.

BONE MEASUREMENTS

It was possible to measure several skeletal elements. The bone measurements are useful for comparing the animal population, especially the domestic ones kept at various archaeological sites within a cultural ambience or between sites of different cultures (Joglekar 1993, 1996, 2000-2001). At present comparative material from other archaeological sites is scanty, except the medieval site of Kelshi located several hundred kilometres south of Sanjan (Joglekar *et al.* 1996-1997, 2001-2002). Yet the actual measurements are given in tables 15-** along with the appropriate standard measurement codes followed in archaeozoological research. These measurements could be used in future when faunal material from other sites contemporary to Sanjan would be available.

Table 13 Sanjan-B: Distribution of skeletal elements of spotted deer

Skeletal Type\Layer	2	3	4	5	6	7	Total
Head	0	0	1	0	0	0	1
Axial	0	0	0	0	0	0	0
Forequarter	0	1	2	1	4	1	9
Hindquarter	1	1	3	1	1	2	9
Fore foot	0	0	0	0	0	0	0
Hind foot	0	0	0	0	0	0	0
Foot	0	0	1	1	0	0	2

Table 14 Sanjan-B: Distribution of skeletal elements of "antelopes"

Skeletal Type\Layer	1	2	3	4	5	6	7	Total
Head	0	2	4	8	1	2	0	17
Axial	0	0	0	0	1	0	0	1
Forequarter	0	0	1	2	1	3	1	8
Hindquarter	0	1	0	4	1	3	1	10
Fore foot	0	0	0	0	0	0	0	0
Hind foot	1	0	1	4	1	0	0	7
Foot	0	0	0	5	0	0	0	5

FAUNAL REMAINS FROM SANJAN

P.P. JOGLEKAR

NOVEMBER 2003

Plate IX

CONCLUDING REMARKS

The detailed study of the faunal remains from Sanjan showed that people at Sanjan had used a wide spectrum of animal resources. They have relied more on the domestic animals such as cattle, sheep, goat, buffalo, pig and domestic fowl than the wild animals and aquatic fauna. Although the proportion of wild mammals exploited for food is small, the species diversity is impressive. People at Sanjan have hunted nilgai, gazelle, four-horned antelope and blackbuck that are typical semi-arid species; two deer species; large bovids such as gaur and wild buffalo; and small mammalian species like hare, squirrel and mongoose. A good degree of difference (Jaccard's Coefficient of Dissimilarity = 0.45) has been observed between the mammalian fauna at

SJN-B and SJN-K. The wolf; large bovids (gaur and wild buffalo) and gazelles were absent in the faunal collection from SJN-K. The study of the total faunal assemblage from SJN-K and a sample of assemblage from SJN-B revealed a complete picture of medieval economy with its component of animal-based subsistence, animals used for transport and dog as a watch animal.

ACKNOWLEDGEMENTS

I wish to thank Dr. S.P. Gupta and his team for entrusting the faunal material to me. Such kind of work is only possible when the excavators treat the animal bones with due care like it has been done at Sanjan. I thank Dr. P.K. Thomas to whom I went several times whenever I had problems

Table 15 Sanjan: measurements of fore limb bones

Humerus

REG_NO	TRENCH	LAYER	DEPTH	SPECIES	GL	Bp	Tp	Bd
SJN081	B4-SW	*18	Pit	*Boselaphus tragocamelus*	--	--	--	51.76
SJN285	TT1NW	4	1.61	*Bandicota indica*	38.65		--	11.63
SJN307	TT1NW	3	1.18	*Antilope cervicapra*	--	--	--	29.50
SJN215	TT1SW	6	3.35	*Antilope cervicapra*	--	35.4	20.00	--
SJN205	TT1SW	7	3.62	*Antilope cervicapra*	--	--	--	29.67

GL: Maximum Length
Bp: Maximum proximal width
Tp: Proximal thickness
Bd: Maximum distal width

Radius

REG_NO	TRENCH	LAYER	DEPTH	SPECIES	GL	Bp	BFp	Wd
SJN247	TT2SE	4	1.57	*Antilope cervicapra*	--	--	--	31.56
SJN214	TT1SW	6	3.35	*Axis axis*	--	--	--	30.60
SJN216	TT1SW	6	3.25	*Axis axis*	--	33.90	18.41	--

Bp: Maximum proximal width
BFp: Width of the proximal articular surface
Bd: Maximum distal width
Wd: Width of the distal articular surface

Ulna

REG_NO	TRENCH	LAYER	DEPTH	SPECIES	GL	BPC
SJN212	TT1SW	6	3.35	*Antilope cervicapra*	--	22.41
SJN219	TT1SW	6	--	*Axis axis*	--	18.76

GL: Maximum Length
BPC: Width of the articular surface

Table 16 Sanjan: measurements of hind limb bones

Femur

REG_NO	TRENCH	LAYER	DEPTH	SPECIES	GL	Bp	TC	Bd
SJN235	TT2SW	4	1.72	*Ovis aries*	--	--	21.16	--
SJN269	TT1NW	4	1.61	*Capra hircus* (domestic)	--	--	22.38	--
SJN286	TT1NW	4	1.61	*Bandicota indica*	57.86	13.75	--	11.57
SJN287	TT1NW	4	1.61	*Bandicota indica*	57.42	14.29	--	11.76

GL : Maximum Length
Bp : Maximum proximal width
GLC : *Length of the capitulum*
TC : Width of the capitulum
Bd : Maximum distal width

Tibia

REG_NO	TRENCH	LAYER	DEPTH	SPECIES	GL	Bp	Bd	Td
SJN283	TT1NW	4	1.61	*Bandicota indica*	56.00	--	7.10	7.40
SJN284	TT1NW	4	1.61	*Bandicota indica*	56.90	--	6.93	7.41

GL: Maximum Length
Bp: Maximum proximal width
Bd: Maximum distal width
Td: Maximum distal thickness

Table 17 Sanjan: measurements of first phalanges

REG_NO	TRENCH	LAYER	DEPTH	SPECIES	GL	Bp	Tp	Bd
SJN273	TT2SE	4	1.72	*Gazella bennetti*	--	--	--	12.95
SJN006	A3-SW	3	0.64	*Capra hircus* (domestic)	43.90	15.80	18.36	14.05
SJN302	TT2SE	3	1.24	*Capra hircus* (domestic)	--	--	--	13.18
SJN303	TT2SE	3	1.24	*Capra hircus* (domestic)	--	--	--	14.81
SJN274	TT2SE	4	1.72	*Boselaphus tragocamelus*	54.05	17.00	18.46	15.50
SJN014	A4-SW	1	0.18	*Bos indicus*	47.95	22.64	25.38	20.90
SJN029	A3-SE	1	0.30	*Bos indicus*	49.11	20.29	25.00	20.00
SJN049	A3-NE	1	0.18	*Bos indicus*	50.10	22.11	28.11	22.83
SJN058	B4-NE	1	0.08	*Bos indicus*	49.55	21.90	22.37	19.75
SJN113	BAULK	*16	--	*Bos indicus*	46.68	18.94	22.00	19.15
SJN114	BAULK	*16	--	*Bos indicus*	44.10	19.00	21.10	18.61
SJN117	BAULK	*16	--	*Bos indicus*	46.05	21.00	21.55	19.84
SJN118	BAULK	*16	--	*Bos indicus*	47.05	20.00	22.08	18.34
SJN095	B5-SW	*19	Pit	*Bos indicus*	--	--	13.20	--
SJN094	B3-NE	3	0.57	*Axis axis*	39.43	14.30	16.36	12.72
SJN227	TT2SE	5	2.56	*Axis axis*	--	--	--	13.71
SJN249	TT2SE	4	1.57	*Antilope cervicapra*	36.35	11.95	14.56	11.68
SJN257	TT2SE	4	1.57	*Antilope cervicapra*	--	--	--	13.10
SJN276	TT2SE	4	1.45	*Antilope cervicapra*	--	--	--	12.33

GL: *Maximum length*
Bp: Maximum proximal width
Tp: Proximal thickness
Bd: *Maximum distal width*

Table 18 Sanjan: measurements of second and third phalanges

Second phalanges

REG_NO	TRENCH	LAYER	DEPTH	SPECIES	GL	Bp	Tp	Bd
SJN007	A3-SW	2	0.48	*Ovis aries*	--	13.05	12.42	--
SJN234	TT2SW	4	1.72	*Ovis aries*	--	11.55	11.45	--
SJN008	A3-SW	2	0.48	*Capra hircus* (domestic)	35.73	15.34	22.00	11.82
SJN272	TT2SE	4	1.72	*Capra hircus* (domestic)	22.11	12.00	13.40	9.45
SJN093	B3-NE	3	0.57	*Bubalus bubalis*	35.32	25.04	26.50	23.40
SJN123	BAULK	*17	Pit	*Bubalus bubalis*	32.64	18.67	22.94	15.47
SJN344	TT1SW	1	0.76	*Bubalus arnee*	48.83	35.84	--	31.00
SJN320	TT2SE	2	0.88	*Bubalus arnee*	53.44	36.10	37.11	30.11
SJN027	A3-SE	1	0.30	*Bos indicus*	30.02	21.26	23.00	17.10
SJN028	A3-SE	1	0.30	*Bos indicus*	29.94	20.50	22.13	17.21
SJN050	A3-NE	1	0.18	*Bos indicus*	34.38	23.37	26.53	19.13
SJN059	B4-NE	1	0.08	*Bos indicus*	30.10	19.82	21.31	17.20
SJN060	B4-NE	1	0.08	*Bos indicus*	--	20.00	22.50	--
SJN083	A3-NW	3	0.66	*Bos indicus*	33.24	23.28	24.66	20.41
SJN115	BAULK	*16	--	*Bos indicus*	31.60	20.13	22.30	18.25
SJN116	BAULK	*16	--	*Bos indicus*	30.75	19.80	21.90	18.15
SJN119	BAULK	*16	--	*Bos indicus*	30.62	19.16	21.00	15.24
SJN047	A3-SE	1	0.35	*Axis axis*	31.92	15.21	19.45	11.86
SJN067	A3-NE	2	0.42	*Axis axis*	31.43	14.65	17.12	11.38
SJN232	TT2SW	4	1.72	*Axis axis*	30.53	13.05	13.40	10.25

GL: *Maximum length*
Bp: Maximum proximal width
Tp: Proximal thickness
Bd: *Maximum distal width*

Third phalanges

REG_NO	TRENCH	LAYER	DEPTH	SPECIES	1	2	3
SJN254	TT2SE	4	1.57	*Capra hircus* (domestic)	--	--	10.15
SJN255	TT2SE	4	1.57	*Capra hircus* (domestic)	29.41	23.06	9.45
SJN256	TT2SE	4	1.57	*Capra hircus* (domestic)	31.27	26.18	10.84
SJN120	BAULK	*16	--	*Bos indicus*	--	--	16.64
SJN125	BAULK	*17	Pit	*Bos indicus*	--	--	14.68
SJN126	BAULK	*17	Pit	*Bos indicus*	--	--	15.37

1 :Maximum length
2 :Dorsal length
3 :Width of the articular surface

Table 19 Sanjan: measurements of tarsals and carpals

Astragalus

REG_NO	TRENCH	LAYER	DEPTH	SPECIES	GLl	GLm	Bd	Dl	Dm
SJN319	TT2SE	2	0.88	*Ovis aries*	31.18	--	18.40	--	--
SJN051	A3-NE	1	0.18	*Cervus unicolor*	--	--	36.00	--	--
SJN048	A3-SW	1	0.22	*Bos indicus*	60.82	57.90	38.72	31.90	--
SJN282	TT2SE	4	1.45	*Antilope cervicapra*	29.25	27.30	18.00	--	--

GLl: Lateral Length
GLm :   Medial length
Bd: Maximum distal width
Dl: Maximum lateral thickness
Dm: Maximum medial thickness

Calcaneum

REG_NO	TRENCH	LAYER	DEPTH	SPECIES	1	2	3
SJN054	A3-SW	1	0.36	*Bos indicus*	--	28.20	40.00
SJN112	A3-NW	2	0.56	*Bos indicus*	--	38.60	46.00
SJN208	TT1SW	7	3.62	*Capra hircus* (domestic)	--	24.35	16.83

1 :   Maximum Length
2 :   Maximum Width
3 :   Maximum Height

Centrotarsal

REG_NO	TRENCH	LAYER	DEPTH	SPECIES	Maximum width
SJN086	B4-NW	1	0.24	*Axis axis*	31.74

Magnum

REG_NO	TRENCH	LAYER	DEPTH	SPECIES	1	2	3
SJN124	BAULK	*17	Pit	*Bubalus bubalis*	23.33	23.00	15.00
SJN017	A4-SW	1	0.18	*Bos indicus*	26.00	25.38	13.86
SJN315	TT1-NE	2	0.83	*Bos indicus*	38.95	36.24	21.36

1 :   Maximum Length
2 :   Maximum Width
3 :   Maximum Thickness

Table 20 Sanjan: measurements of mandibles and maxillae

Bone	Measurement	Maxilla	Mandible	Mandible
REG_NO		SJN039	SJN078	SJN111
TRENCH		A4-SW (1)	B4-NE (1)	A3-NW (2)
DEPTH		0.35	0.30	0.56
SPECIES		*Sus domesticus*	*Capra hircus* (domestic)	*Sus domesticus*
dp4	Length	--	--	15.00
	Width	--	--	7.30
P3	Length	11.64	--	--
	Width	7.87	--	--
M1	Length	13.95	--	--
	Width	11.34	--	--
M2	Length	18.29	--	--
	Width	14.73	--	--
M1	Length	13.95	--	--
	Width	11.34	--	--
M2	Length	18.29	--	--
	Width	14.73	--	--
M3	Length	--	21.45	--
	Width	--	12.12	--

Table 21 Sanjan: measurements of isolated maxillary teeth

REG_NO	TRENCH	LAYER	DEPTH	TOOTH	SPECIES	LENGTH	WIDTH
SJN046	A4-NW	1	0.37	M0	*Bos indicus*	29.14	13.10
SJN229	TT2SW	4	1.72	M1	*Capra hircus* (domestic)	17.56	12.58
SJN130	A5-SW	1	0.33	M1	*Equus asinus*	25.35	29.90
SJN080	B4-NW	1	0.28	M2	*Antilope cervicapra*	15.05	14.50
SJN309	TT1NW	3	1.18	M2	*Antilope cervicapra*	18.44	9.45
SJN252	TT2SE	4	1.57	M2	*Antilope cervicapra*	15.10	12.28
SJN261	TT1SW	4	2.23	M2	*Antilope cervicapra*	19.55	13.00
SJN209	TT1SW	6	3.61	M2	*Antilope cervicapra*	17.16	9.71
SJN003	B4-NE	1	0.32	M2	*Axis axis*	19.00	14.95
SJN084	B4-NE	2	0.36	M2	*Axis axis*	19.00	12.75
SJN105	B4-NW	2	0.32	M2	*Axis axis*	16.80	13.86
SJN298	TT1SW	3	0.95	M2	*Bos gaurus*	28.75	28.32
SJN032	A4-SE	1	0.27	M2	*Bos indicus*	23.00	18.00
SJN034	A4-SE	1	0.27	M2	*Bos indicus*	23.00	18.10
SJN348	TT1SW	1	0.57	M2	*Bos indicus*	24.44	24.62
SJN343	TT2SW	1	0.68	M2	*Bubalus bubalis*	24.85	17.55
SJN345	TT1SW	1	0.76	M2	*Bubalus bubalis*	26.00	25.88
SJN351	TT1SW	1	0.57	M2	*Bubalus bubalis*	28.32	28.00
SJN043	A4-SE	2	1.00	M2	*Capra hircus* (domestic)	15.13	12.30
SJN278	TT2SE	4	1.45	M2	Capra hircus (domestic)	16.77	8.82
SJN339	TT1	1	BAULK	M2	*Capra hircus* (domestic)	17.25	9.50
SJN311	TT1NW	3	1.18	M2	*Tetracerus quadricornis*	15.50	7.37
SJN337	TT1	1	BAULK	M2	*Tetracerus quadricornis*	13.15	14.00
SJN035	B3-NE	1	0.16	M3	*Axis axis*	23.65	12.85
SJN069	A4-NW	1	0.19	M3	*Axis axis*	24.50	14.93
SJN033	A4-SE	1	0.27	M3	*Bos indicus*	25.16	18.00
SJN352	TT1SW	1	0.57	M3	*Bubalus bubalis*	32.53	22.30
SJN224	TT2SE	5	2.68	M3	*Bubalus bubalis*	33.12	22.80
SJN098	A4-SW	1	0.22	M3	*Capra hircus* (domestic)	15.73	9.15

REG_NO	TRENCH	LAYER	DEPTH	TOOTH	SPECIES	LENGTH	WIDTH
SJN297	TT1SW	3	0.95	M3	Capra hircus (domestic)	17.22	10.28
SJN308	TT1NW	3	1.18	M3	Capra hircus (domestic)	17.65	12.00
SJN260	TT1SW	4	2.23	M3	Capra hircus (domestic)	17.92	10.00
SJN066	B5-SW	*21	BAULK	M3	Capra hircus (domestic)	20.05	12.55
SJN250	TT2SE	4	1.57	P2	Antilope cervicapra	10.54	9.65
SJN335	TT1SW	1	0.62	P2	Bos indicus	17.64	19.50
SJN321	TT2SE	2	0.71	P2	Bos indicus	19.55	19.05
SJN328	TT1SE	2	0.72	P2	Bos indicus	28.00	17.45
SJN305	TT1NE	3	0.96	P2	Bos indicus	18.60	14.55
SJN015	A4-SW	1	0.18	P2	Boselaphus tragocamelus	13.18	16.85
SJN127	A5-SW	1	0.33	P2	Equus asinus	27.92	20.36
SJN277	TT2SE	4	1.45	P2	Ovis aries	9.31	8.92
SJN103	A4-SW	*23	0.53	P3	Axis axis	12.43	11.44
SJN064	A3-NW	*21	BAULK	P3	Bos indicus	17.33	16.75
SJN128	A5-SW	1	0.33	P3	Equus asinus	20.93	20.94

Table 22 Sanjan: measurements of isolated mandibular teeth

REG_NO	TRENCH	LAYER	DEPTH	TOOTH	SPECIES	LENGTH	WIDTH
SJN092	A5-NE	1	0.44	d3	Bos indicus	8.46	6.10
SJN088	A5-NE	1	0.44	d4	Bos indicus	18.67	8.54
SJN089	A5-NE	1	0.44	i1	Bos indicus	8.74	7.62
SJN090	A5-NE	1	0.44	i1	Bos indicus	8.00	8.00
SJN091	A5-NE	1	0.44	i1	Bos indicus	8.78	6.41
SJNxxx	A5-SW	1	0.20	i1	Boselaphus tragocamelus	9.14	6.78
SJN258	TT2SE	4	1.57	i1	Capra hircus (domestic)	5.75	4.46
SJN326	TT1SE	2	0.72	i3	Bos gaurus	18.60	10.70
SJN304	TT1NE	3	0.96	i3	Bos gaurus	17.87	10.20
SJNxx1	A4-SE	1	0.27	i3	Bos indicus	13.65	7.65
SJN325	TT2SE	2	0.85	m1	Bos indicus	24.43	17.00
SJN327	TT1SE	2	0.72	m1	Bos indicus	21.00	22.44
SJN301	TT2SE	3	1.24	m1	Bos indicus	30.00	14.82
SJN259	TT1SW	4	2.23	m1	Capra hircus (domestic)	18.65	8.90
SJN231	TT2SW	4	1.72	m1	Gazella bennetti	12.50	8.65
SJN262	TT1SW	4	2.23	m1	Gazella bennetti	15.70	10.00
SJN329	TT1NW	2	0.90	m2	Antilope cervicapra	9.12	8.15
SJN268	TT1NW	4	1.61	m2	Antilope cervicapra	17.40	11.20
SJN223	TT2SE	5	2.61	m2	Antilope cervicapra	18.05	9.73
SJN338	TT1	1	BAULK	m3	Antilope cervicapra	22.00	8.56
SJN340	TT1	1	BAULK	m3	Bos indicus	37.90	16.00
SJN310	TT1NW	3	1.18	m3	Capra hircus (domestic)	23.55	7.57
SJN266	TT1NW	4	1.61	m3	Capra hircus (domestic)	21.62	8.44
SJN349	TT1SW	1	0.57	m3	Capra hircus/Ovis aries	20.16	7.84
SJN350	TT1SW	1	0.57	m3	Capra hircus/Ovis aries	23.51	8.13
SJN279	TT2SE	4	1.45	m3	Tetracerus quadricornis	23.71	9.60
SJN018	A4-SW	1	0.18	p2	Axis axis	13.70	10.50
SJN052	A3-NE	1	0.18	p2	Bos indicus	9.35	7.05
SJN230	TT2SW	4	1.72	p2	Gazella bennetti	7.75	5.75
SJN331	TT1SW	1	0.40	p4	Bos indicus	21.05	14.45
SJN332	TT1SW	1	0.40	p4	Bos indicus	20.68	12.67
SJN333	TT1SW	1	0.40	p4	Bos indicus	21.76	13.24
SJN129	A5-SW	1	0.33	P4	Equus asinus	21.29	19.90
SJN312	TT1NW	3	1.18	p4	Tetracerus quadricornis	11.18	7.10

Table 23 Sanjan: measurements (diameter) of fish vertebrae

REG-NO	TRENCH	LAYER	DEPTH	TAXONOMIC UNIT	WIDTH	HEIGHT
SJN318	TT1NE	2	0.83	Marine Fish (small)	8.60	8.75
SJN313	TT1NW	3	1.18	Marine Fish (small)	8.80	9.10
SJN270	TT1NW	4	1.61	Marine Fish (small)	10.00	9.46
SJN076	B4-SW	1	0.12	Marine Fish (medium)	10.66	10.40
SJN075	B4-SW	1	0.12	Marine Fish (medium)	10.80	12.00
SJN316	TT1NE	2	0.83	Marine Fish (medium)	10.90	11.15
SJN263	TT1SW	4	2.23	Marine Fish (medium)	10.95	11.90
SJN074	B4-SW	1	0.12	Marine Fish (medium)	11.10	11.90
SJN110	A3-SW	2	0.52	Marine Fish (medium)	11.70	13.50
SJN097	A3-NW	3	0.66	Marine Fish (medium)	11.87	11.87
SJN106	B5-SW	2	0.39	Marine Fish (medium)	11.90	14.40
SJN253	TT2SE	4	1.57	Marine Fish (medium)	12.19	12.43
SJN238	TT2SW	4	1.72	Marine Fish (medium)	12.40	12.78
SJN239	TT2SW	4	1.72	Marine Fish (medium)	12.60	12.95
SJN104	B4-NW	1	0.16	Marine Fish (medium)	12.72	12.86
SJN045	A3-SE	2	0.65	Marine Fish (medium)	13.00	14.93
SJN317	TT1NE	2	0.83	Marine Fish (medium)	13.05	13.12
SJN237	TT2SW	4	1.72	Marine Fish (medium)	13.50	13.72
SJN077	B4-SW	1	0.12	Marine Fish (medium)	13.90	16.50
SJN353	TT1SW	1	0.57	Marine Fish (medium)	13.90	15.00
SJN281	TT2SE	4	1.45	Marine Fish (medium)	14.00	13.90
SJN306	TT1NE	3	0.96	Marine Fish (medium)	14.80	14.80
SJN222	TT2SE	5	2.61	Marine Fish (medium)	16.00	17.50
SJN046	A4-SE	1	0.27	Marine Fish (medium)	16.80	17.00
SJN334	TT1SW	1	0.4	Marine Fish (medium)	16.95	17.00
SJN217	TT1SW	6	3.25	Marine Fish (medium)	17.11	16.50
SJN211	TT1SW	6	3.35	Marine Fish (medium)	17.24	19.00
SJN243	TT2SE	4	2.37	Marine Fish (medium)	18.40	18.41
SJN342	TT1	1	BAULK	Marine Fish (medium)	18.44	18.00
SJN341	TT1	1	BAULK	Marine Fish (medium)	19.23	18.85
SJN228	TT1SW	5	3.17	Marine Fish (Large)	20.64	19.17
SJN206	TT1SW	7	3.62	Marine Fish (Large)	24.13	27.30
SJN210	TT1SW	6	3.61	Marine Fish (Large)	26.40	24.61
SJN207	TT1SW	7	3.62	Marine Fish (Large)	--	26.46

in identifying certain skeletal fragments. I am grateful to Drs. Abhijit Dandekar and Kurush Dalal for help in various ways.

REFERENCES

Clason, A.T. 1972. Some Remarks on the Use and Presentation of Archaeozoological Data, *Helinium* 12(2): 139-153.

Gupta, S.P. K.F. Dalal, Abhijit Dandekar, Rhea Mitra, Rukshana Nanji and Rohini Pandey 2002-2003. A Preliminary Report on the Excavations at Sanjan (2002), *Puratattva* 32: 182-198.

Joglekar, P.P. 1990 (unpublished). *Bird Family Identification Criteria*, A report prepared at Biologisch-Archaeologisch Instituut, Groningen, The Netherlands.

Joglekar P.P. 1993. Height at withers: An Osteometric Approach to Faunal Remains, *Bharati* 20: 31-38.

Joglekar P.P. 1996. Faunal Quantification: Review of New Trends, *Puratattva* 26: 1-6.

Joglekar, P.P 2000-2001. Applications of Mathematics and Statistics in Archaeozoological Research: a Review, *Bulletin of the Deccan College Post-graduate Research Institute* 60-61: 109-136.

Joglekar P.P., P.K. Thomas, Y. Matsushima and S.J. Pawankar 1994. Osteological Differences Between the Forelimb Bones of Ox (*Bos indicus*), Buffalo (*Bubalus bubalis*) and Nilgai (*Boselaphus tragocamelus*), *Journal of Bombay Veterinary College* 5 (1-2): 17-20.

Joglekar P.P., Arati Deshpande-Mukherjee and Sharmila Joshi 1996-97. Report on the Faunal Remains from Kelshi, District Ratnagiri, Maharashtra, *Puratattva* 27: 91-95.

Pawankar, S.J. and P.K. Thomas 2001. Osteological Differences between Blackbuck (*Antilope cervicapra*), Goat (*Capra hircus*) and Sheep (*Ovis aries*), *Man and Environment* 26(1): 109-126.

Joglekar, P.P, Sushama Deo, Arati Deshpande-Mukherjee and Savita Ghate 2001-2002. Archaeological Investigation at Kelshi, District Ratnagiri, Maharashtra, *Puratattva* 32: 63-73, 244.

Reitz, E.J. and E.S. Wing 1999. *Archaeozoology*. Cambridge: Cambridge University Press.

Sadek-Kooros, H. 1975. Intentional Fracturing of Bone: Description of Criteria, in *Archaeozoological Studies* (A.T. Clason Ed.), pp. 139-150. Amsterdam: North-Holland Publication.

Schmid, E. 1972. *Atlas of Animal Bones*. Amsterdam: Elsevier.

Uerpmann H-P. 1973. Animal Bone Finds and Economic Archaeology: A Critical Study of Osteo-archaeological Methods, *World Archaeology* 4: 307-322.

Driesch, von A. 1976. *A Guide to the Measurement of Animal Bones from Archaeological Sites*, Cambridge, Massachusetts: Harvard University Press.

CATALOGUE OF COINS FROM THE EXCAVATIONS AT SANJAN (UMBARGAON TALUKA, DISTRICT VALSAD, GUJARAT)

Padmakar Prabhune

Deptt. of History and A.I.H.C.& Archaeology,
Chāndmal Tarāchand Borā College, Shirur – Ghodnadī, Dist. Pune – 412210.
padmakar.prabhune@rediffmail.com

Vijay Sathe

Department of Archaeology,
Deccan College Postgraduate and Research Institute, Pune 411006.
vijay19sathe@gmail.com

Introduction

The excavations at the site of Sanjan were carried out between the year 2002-2004 and, along with a large repertoire of ceramic and other antiquities, a total of seventy eight coins were also recovered (Gupta *et al.* 2002, 2004 & 2005, Nanji and Dhalla 2007, Nanji 2011, Gokhale 2004). The stratigraphical integrity of coins with subsequent chronological frame and typological features assign them a time frame from 5th century A D to Maratha period. Some of them also include coins of lower denominations of British India and present day Indian Republic. The coins belong to Indo-Sassanians, Rashtrakutas, Sultanate and Maratha rulers. The distinct stratigraphic association of the coin assemblage has an important bearing on the socio-political and economic conditions of an early medieval settlement through time. It assumes significance especially when dealing with a (coastal) settlement which is known to have witnessed extensive trade activities for well over a millennium.

Following is the exhaustive catalogue based on total seventy eight coins whose numismatic description offers interesting coordinates of political and economic dimensions with special reference to the site of Sanjan over the period of one thousand years of habitational history.

Catalogue

Abbreviations:

CCC – Commonly available, R – Rare, RRR – Extremely Rare. NA – Not Available
(This categorisation is based on the availability and uniqueness of the particular coin type).
Archaeological provenance of the coin is mentioned in italics. – Location, trench, quadrant, depth, layer, lot no, reg. no.

Coin No. 01

Shape :- Round
Size :- 1.5 cm Diameter
Thickness :- 2 mm (0.2 cm)
Weight :- 3.10 gms.
Metal :- Billon

Obverse   Reverse

Obv. Arabic Legend : *Muhammad bin tughalaq shah*
Rev. *Abul Mujahid fi-sabil allah*
Dynasty :- Delhi Sultan , Tughlaq
King :- Muhammad Tughlaq
Period :- No date on coin, (725 -752 AH) 1325 – 1351 A.D.
Denomination - Six Gani .
Rare : - CCC
Archaeological provenance: *SJN-B 2002, TT1, NE, surface, 1.*
Historical significance :- NA

Coin No. 02

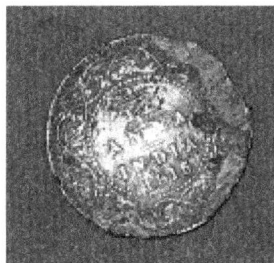

Coin of British India

Shape :- Round
Metal :- Copper
1/12 Anna of 1915 A.D.
Rare : - CCC
Archaeological provenance: *SJN-B 2002, TT1 NE, surface, 1119.*
Historical significance :- NA

Coin No. 03

Shape :- Round
Size :- 1.5 cm diameter
Thickness :- 3 mm (0.3 cm)
Weight :- 2.97 gms.
Metal :- Copper

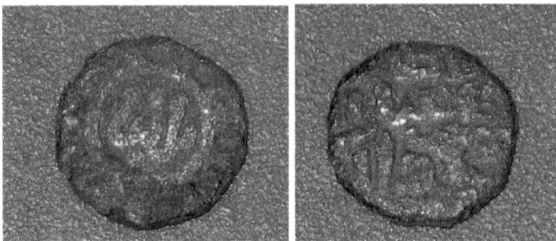

Obverse   Reverse

Obv. Arabic Legend : in circle – *Balban out of circle Sri sultan Gayasadin* .
Rev. *Al sultan al a`zam Ghiyas ud – duniya waddin.*
Dynasty :- Delhi Sultan , Mamluks or so called slaves.
King :- Ghiyas-ud-din Balban
Rare : - CCC
Period :- No date on coin, (664 - 668 AH) 1266 – 1287 A.D.
Archaeological provenance: *SJN-B 2002, TT1 NE, surface, 1118.*
Historical significance :- NA

Coin No. 04

Shape :- Round
Size :- 1.5 cm diameter
Thickness :- 2.5 mm (0.25 cm)
Weight :- 3.19 gms.
Metal :- Alloy base silver

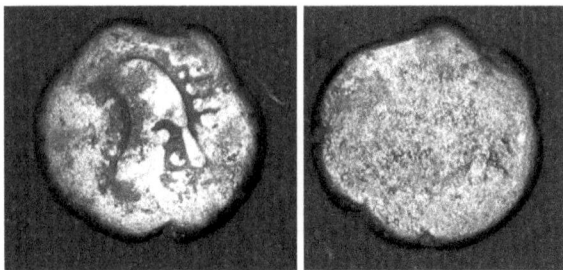

Obverse   Reverse

Obv. Crude face of a king
Rev. Iranian fire alter
Dynasty :- Gadhiya type

King :- ----------?------------
Period :- No date on coin, 6th to 8th Century A.D.
Rare : - CCC
Archaeological provenance: *SJN-B 2002, TT1, SW, 0.40m, 1, 102, 160.*
Historical significance :- NA

Coin No. 05

Shape :- Round
Size :- 1.5 cm diameter
Thickness :- 2.5 mm (0.25 cm)
Weight :- 3.29 gms.
Metal :- Alloy base silver

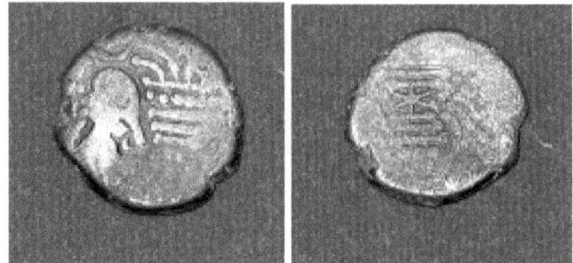

Obverse   Reverse

Obv. Crude face of a king
Rev. Iranian fire alter
Dynasty :- Gadhiya type
King :- ----------?------------
Period :- No date on coin, 6th to 8th Century A.D.
Rare : - CCC
Archaeological provenance: *SJN-B 2002, TT1, SW, 0.40m (l = 0.70m, b = 2m), 1, 102, 161.*
Historical significance :- NA

Coin No. 06

Copper, completely corroded, beyond identification.
Archaeological provenance: *SJN_B 2002, TT1,SW, 1.59m, 3,140,1060.*

Coin No. 07

Shape :- Round small
Size :- 1.2 cm diameter
Thickness :- 0.5 mm (0.05 cm)
Weight :- 0.35 gms.
Metal :- Silver

Obverse   Reverse

Amir of Sindh Ruler: (870 – 1030 A.D.)
Ruler (Amir):Umar
Obv. In kufic calligraphy; *Allah yasiq umar wa fansar*
Rev. In Kufic calligraphy *Allah Muhammad rasul allah Umar.*
Dynasty :- Amirs of Sindh
Period :- No date on coin, (870 – 1030 A.D)
Rare : - R
Archaeological provenance: *SJN-B 2002, TT1, SW, 1.16m, 3, 137,1045.*
Historical significance :- Coin of Amirs of Sindh

Coin No. 08

Shape :- Round
Size :- 1.5 cm diameter
Thickness :- 0.5 mm (0.05 cm)
Weight :- 0.47 gms.
Metal :- Copper

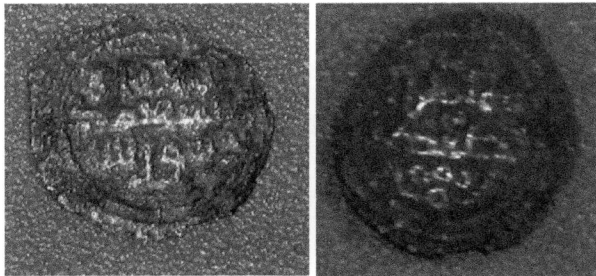

Obverse   Reverse

Amirs of Sindh (870 – 1030 A.D.) ? or Arab Governor of Sind. (712 – 870 A.D.)
Legend worn out traces of *rasul allah* on obv.
Period :- No date visible on coin,
Rare : - RR
Archaeological provenance: *SJNTT1, SE, 0.63m, 2, 707, 80.*
Historical significance :- The coin type resembles with those of the type of Arab Governors of Sind.

Coin No. 09

Copper , Completely corroded , beyond identification.
Archaeological provenance: *SJN_B 2002, TT1,SE, 1.79m, 3, 715, 1134.*

Coin No. 10

Shape :- Round
Size :- 1.5 cm diameter
Thickness :- 4 mm (0.4 cm)
Weight :- 3.39 gms.
Metal :- Alloy with silver

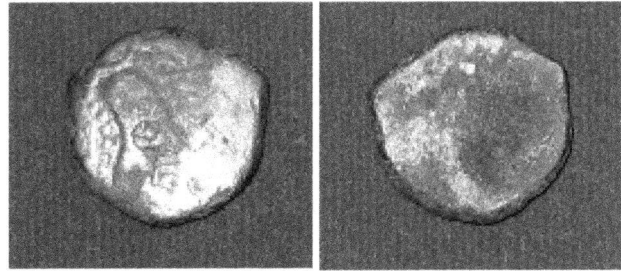

Obverse   Reverse

Obv. Crude face of a king
Rev. Iranian fire alter but corroded
Dynasty :- Gadhiya type
King :- ----------------------
Period :- No date on coin, 6th century A.D. onwards.
Rare : - CCC
Archaeological provenance: *SJN-B 2002, TT1, NE, 0.46m, 1 ,502, 45.*
Historical significance :- NA

Coin No. 11

Shape :- Round
Size :- 1.6 cm Diameter
Thickness :- 2 mm (0.2 cm)
Weight :- 2.46 gms.
Metal :- Copper

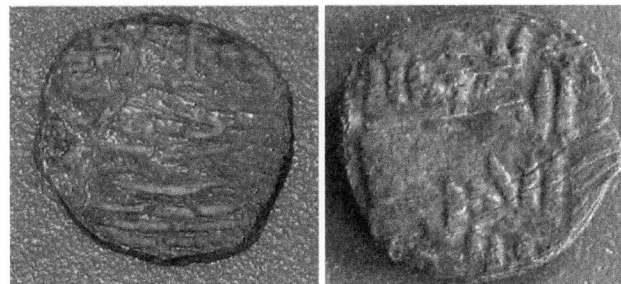

Obverse   Reverse

Obv. A seated figure probably of a garuda, two swastika symbols , one reverse swastika.
Rev. Arabic legends probably reads, *Al sultan or al malik*
Dynasty :- Rashtrakutas ? (as can be identified on the basis of Garuda Mudra on Rashtrakuta copper plates.)
King :- ------------------------
Period :- No date on coin, 700 – 900 A.D.
Rare : - RRR
Archaeological provenance: *SJN-B 2002, TT!, NE, 0.57m, 1, 503, 68.*

Historical significance :- First Known coins of this type, extremely rare types, unique for depicting human or anthropomorphic figure of Garuda with swastika with Arabic legend.

Similar type of coins were also issued by the Arab Governors of Sind, (712 – 870 A.D.). The coins have six pointed stars within geometric pattern, formed by two overlapping squares on one side and the name of the governor on other (Goron and Goenka 2001: xxii).

Coin No. 12

Shape :- Round
Size :- 2 cm Diameter
Thickness :- 4 mm (0.4 cm)
Weight :- 9.02 gms.
Metal :- Copper

Obv. Devanagari legend – *(Sri) / ra ja*
Rev. *chha (tra) / pa ti.*
Dynasty :- Marathas, Peshwa period.
King :- Peshwa period.
Period :- No date on coin, 1700-1800 A.D.
Rare : - CCC
Archaeological provenance: *SJN –B 2004, surface, 2350.*
Historical significance :- Maratha coin.

Coin No. 13

Copper, Completely corroded, unidentifiable.

Archaeological provenance: *SJN –B 2002, TT1, NE, 0.71m, 2, 504, 103.*

Coin No. 14

Shape :- Round (the coin is broken, a piece of coin)
Size :- full coin would have been of 3 cm Diameter
Thickness :- 0.5 mm (0.05 cm)
Weight :- 0.75 gms.
Metal :- Silver

Obverse   Reverse

Obv. Arabic legends in Kufic style
Rev. Arabic legends

Dynasty :- Abbasid or Iranian.
King :- ------------------------
Period :- No date on coin, 700 – 900 A.D.?
Rare : - RRR
Archaeological provenance: *SJN-2002, TT1, NE, 1.04m (l = 3.20m, b = 3.32m), 3, 512, 243.*

Historical significance :- This may be a fragment of a Dinar from Iran. However, the identification stands open to revision. Only the traces of Arabic legend in kufic style are visible.

Coin No. 15

Shape :- Round (broken)
Size :- 0.9 cm diameter
Thickness :- 0.5 mm (0.05 cm)
Weight :- 0.14 gms.
Metal :- Silver

Obverse   Reverse

Obv. Elephant to right , with small tail,
Rev. Post Gupta Brahmi legends :- *(shri) A mo / { gha} va sa*
Dynasty :- Rashtrakutas
King :- Amoghvarsha
Period :- No date on coin, 700 – 900 A.D.
Rare : - RRR
Archaeological provenance: *SJN-B 2002, TT1, NE, 1.04m (l = 3.80m, b = 3.14m), 3, 512, 242.*
Historical significance :- First Known coins of this type, extreme rare, legend reads *Amo(gha)varsha.* Hitherto only two Rashtrakuta coins have been reported. This happens to be the third one and the first of king Amoghvarsha. Very few Rashtrakuta coins have come to light so far. The two known coins which have been described by Bhandare (2000: 4) were issued by the kings, Dhruva and Karkaraja.

Coin No. 16

Shape :- Round (broken)
Size :- 0.9 cm diameter
Thickness :- 0.2 mm (0.02 cm)
Weight :- gms.
Metal :- Silver

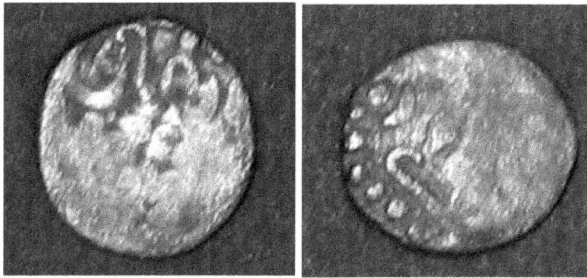

Obverse	Reverse

Obv. Brahmi legends *Shri ran a or shm ka ra*
Rev. may be a portrait
Dynasty :- Kalchuri ? / Trikutaka ? Uncertain
King :- ?
Period :- No date on coin 600 – 700 A.D. (dating based on palaeographic grounds)
Rare : - RRR
Archaeological provenance: *SJN- B 2002TT1, NE, 1.24m, 3, 517, 980.*
Historical significance :- First Known coins of this type, extreme rare.

Coin No. 17

Shape :- Round
Size :- 2 cm diameter
Thickness :- 4 mm (0.4 cm)
Weight :- 8.46 gms.
Metal :- Copper

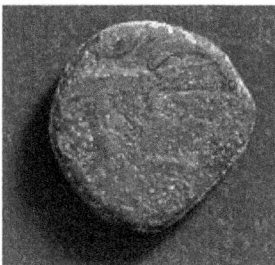

Obv. *(Shri) ra ja ,*
Rev. *Chha tra / pa ti .*
Dynasty :- Marathas
King :- Peshwa Period.
Period :- No date on coin, 1700-1800 A.D.
Rare : - CCC
Archaeological provenance: *SJN_B 2002, TT1, NW, 13.*
Historical significance :- NA

Coin No. 18

Copper, coin-like object but not a coin.
Archaeological provenance: *SJN-B 2002, TT1, Nw, 1.07m, 3, 318, 738.*

Coin No. 19

Shape :- Round
Size :- 1.5 cm diameter
Thickness :- 4 mm (0.4 cm)

Weight :- 4.04 gms.
Metal :- alloy with silver

Obv. Crude face of a king
Rev. Iranian fire alter
Dynasty :- Gadhiya type
King :- ----------------------
Period :- No date on coin, 6th to 8th Century A.D.
Rare : - CCC
Archaeological provenance: *SJN-B 2002, TT1, NW, 1.18m, 3, 321, 800.*
Historical significance :- Early Gadhiya coin , fine condition.

Coin No. 20

Copper, completely corroded, beyond identification.
Archaeological provenance: *SJN-B 2002,TT2, SW, 0.66m, 1, 903, 335.*

Coin No. 21

Copper, completely corroded , beyond identification. 0.36 gms weight. Probably not a coin.
Archaeological provenance: *SJN-B 2002, TT2, SW, 0.74m, 2, 905, 343.*

Coin No. 22

Lead, Completely corroded , beyond identification. 0.36 gms weight. Probably not a coin.
Archaeological provenance: *SJN-B 2002, TT2, SW, 0.74m, 2, 905, 344.*

Coin No. 23

Shape:- Irregular Round
Size:- 0.7 cm diameter
Thickness:- 0.05 mm (0.005 cm)
Weight:- 0.10 gms.
Metal:- Silver

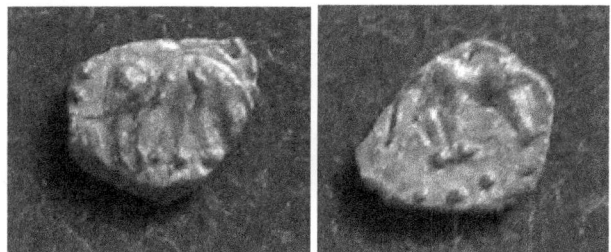

Obv. Elephant to left with tail in normal position.
Rev. Bull or horse to right , tail in normal position, in dotted
   border.
Dynasty :- Kalchuri type or Traikutaka
King :- -------------------------
Period :- No date on coin, 400 – 500 A.D.
Rare : - RRR
Archaeological provenance: *SJN-B 2002, TT2, SW, 1.17m,
   3, 913, 389.*
Historical significance :- Konkan coastal Kalchuri type
   coin. This type of coins were issued by the Kshtrapas.
   Looking at the fabric , it appears to be the post Kshtrapa
   coin. Valuable insights are available on the elephant and
   rider type coins from Handa and Gupta (2003: 3-4).

Coin No. 24

Copper, May be a coin, uncertain, corroded .
Archaeological provenance: *SJN-B 2002, TT2, SE, 0.81m,
   2, 1509, 401.*

Coin No. 25

Shape :- Round
Size :- 1.6 cm diameter
Thickness :- 0.05 mm (0.2 cm)
Weight :- 0.80 gms.
Metal :- Copper

Obv. A seated figure probably a garuda , two swastika
   symbols , one reverse swastik
Rev. Arabic legends probably *Al sultan or al malik*
Dynasty :- Rashtrakutas ? (based on the Garuda Mudra on
   Rashtrakuta copper plates)
King :- -------not knwon------------------
Period :- No date on coin, 700 – 900 A.D.
Rare : - RRR
Archaeological provenance: *SJN-B 2002, TT2, SE, 0.81m,
   2, 1509, 399.*
Historical significance :- First Known coins of this type,
   extreme rare, unique human or anthropomorphic figure
   of Garuda with swastika and Arabic legend.

Similar type of coins were also issued by the Arab
Governors of Sind, (712 – 870 ACE), which describe
six pointed stars within geometric pattern formed by
two overlapping squares on one side and the name of the
governor on other (Goron and Goenka 2001: xxii).

Coin No. 26

Lead, this coin- like object. Completely effaced.
Archaeological provenance: *SJN-B 2002, TT2, SE, 1.52m,
   3, 1522, 662.*

Coin No. 27

Shape :- Round
Size :- 1.5 cm diameter
Thickness :- 2 mm (0.2 cm)
Weight :- 3.64 gms.
Metal :- alloy with silver

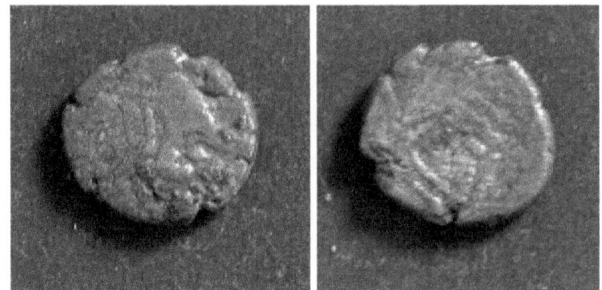

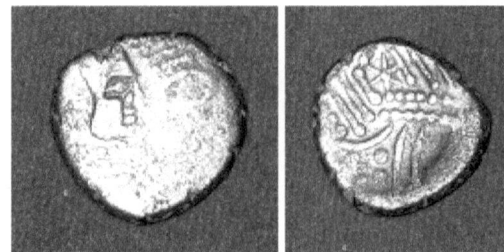

Obv. Crude face of a king with nagari *sri*
Rev. traces of Iranian fire alter
Dynasty :- Gadhiya type
King :- ---------not known------------
Period :- No date on coin, 6th century A.D. onwards. Later
   Gadhiya
Rare : - CCC
Archaeological provenance: *SJN-B 2002, TT2, SE, 1.52m,
   3, 1522, 563*
Historical significance :- NA

Coin No. 28

Shape :- Round
Size :- 1.6 cm diameter
Thickness :- 2 mm (0.2cm)
Weight :- 3.61 gms.
Metal :- alloy with silver

Obv. Crude face of a king
Rev. Iranian fire alter
Dynasty :- Gadhiya type
King :- --------not known--------------
Period :- No date on coin, 6th century onwards.
Rare : - CCC
Archaeological provenance: *SJN-B 2002, TT2, SE, 1.67m,
   4, 1525, 607.*
Historical significance :- NA

Coin No. 29

Shape :- Squire - Round
Size :- 1.5 * 1.4 cm diameter
Thickness :- 2.5 mm
Weight :- 2.92 gms.
Metal :- Copper

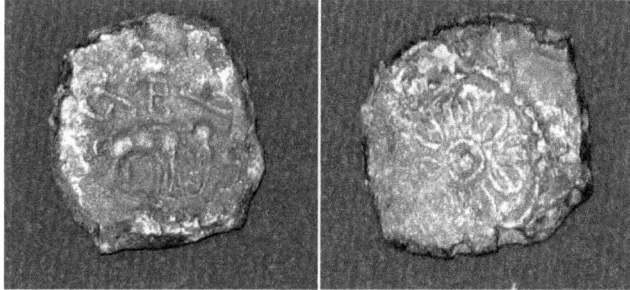

Obv. Elephant to right with tail in normal position. Brahmi legends
Shri (Ra) ja Shra Ya
Rev. Nicely carved lotus of eight petals in dotted circle.
Dynasty :- Uncertain, Kalchuri type
King :- ----------not known---------------
Period :- No date on coin, 500 -600 ACE on paleographic grounds.
Rare : - RRR
Archaeological provenance: *SJN-B 2002, TT2, SE, 2.01m, 4, 1532, 688.*
Historical significance :- Unique hitherto unnoticed type, rare kalchuri type series. Brahmi of Post Gupta period. Eight petal lotus shows Vaishnavite influence i.e. eight petals (Ashtadal Kamal is also seen on the Padmatanka coins of Yadavas of Devagiri)

Coin No. 30

Shape :- Round
Size :- 1.5 cm diameter
Thickness :- 2.5 mm (0.25 cm)
Weight :- 2.88 gms.
Metal :- Copper

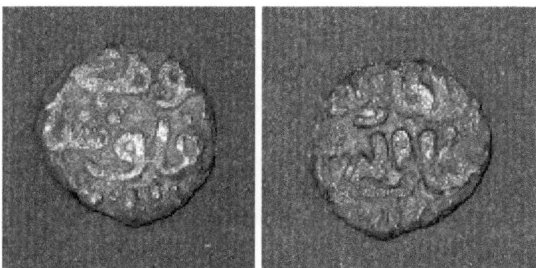

Obverse   Reverse

Obv. *as-sultan al-ghazi ghiyas-ud-duniya waddin*
Rev. *Abul muzaffar Tughlaq shah (al sultan).*
Dynasty :- Delhi Sultan , Tughlaq
King :- Giyasuddin Tughlaq

Period :- No date on coin, (720 – 725 AH) 1320 – 1325 A.D.
Rare : - CCC
Archaeological provenance: *SJN-K 2003, surface, from back filling, 2312.*
Historical significance :- NA

Coin No. 31

Nickel, ½ Anna of 1946 VI George British India. 2.76 grams.
Archaeological provenance: *SJN-K 2003, surface, 2311.*

Coin No. 32

Copper, May be termed as coin.
Archaeological provenance: *SJN-K 2003, surface, 2330.*

Coin No. 33

Shape :- Round
Size :- 0.9 cm diameter
Thickness :- < 1 mm
Weight :- 0.31 gms.
Metal :- Silver

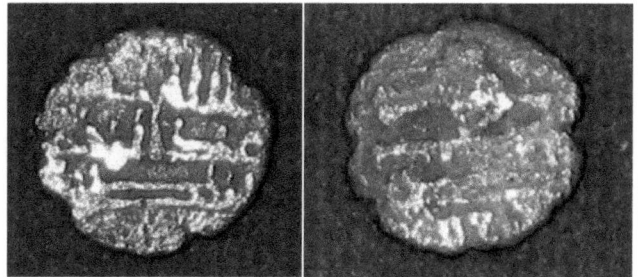

Obv. Arabic Legend : ...
Rev. traces of legend
Dynasty :- Amirs of Sindh
King :- Umar (?)
Period :- date not visible on coin, . 870 – 1030 A.D.
Rare : - R
Archaeological provenance: *SJN-K 2003, surface, 2143.*
Historical significance :- NA

Coin No. 34

Shape :- Round
Size :- 1.6 cm diameter
Thickness :- 5 mm (0.5 mm)
Weight :- 8.64 gms.
Metal :- Copper

Obverse   Reverse

Obv. Traces of *al- amir al-hami*
Rev. *Muhammad shah ---*
Dynasty :- Suri dynasty.
King :- Adil Shah (1552-56 A.D.)
Period :- traces of AH date on coin,
Rare : - CCC
Archaeological provenance: *SJN-K 2003, surface, 2119.*
Historical significance :- NA

Coin No. 35

Copper, completely eroded, may be a coin.
Archaeological provenance: *SJN-K 2003, surface, 1813.*

Coin No. 36

Nickel, British India ½ Anna.
Archaeological provenance: *SJN-K 2003,A3, SE, 0.30m, 1, 3901, 1196.*

Coin No. 37

Copper, completely eroded, may be a coin.
Archaeological provenance: *SJN-K 2003, A3, SE, 0.74m, 3, 3909, 1258.*

Coin No. 38

Copper, badly corroded, beyond identification.
Archaeological provenance: *SJN-K 2003, A4, SW, 0.18m, 1, 4101, 1355.*

Coin No. 39

Shape :- Round
Size :- 2 cm diameter
Thickness :- 5 mm (0.5 mm)
Weight :- 9.77 gms.
Metal :- Copper

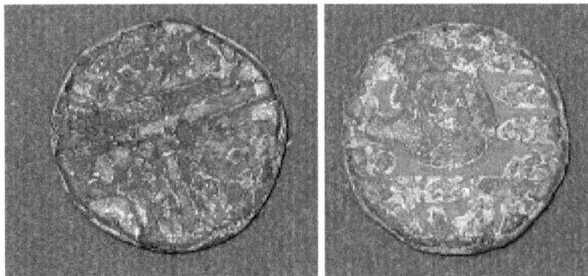

Obv. *Shri ra ja*
Rev. *Chha tra / (pa ti)* .
Shivarai ,later Maratha period.
Dynasty :- Marathas
King :- Peshwa Period.
Period :- No date on coin, 1700-1800 A.D.
Rare : - CCC
Archaeological provenance: *SJN-K 2003, A4, SW, 0.18m, 1, 4101, 1350.*
Historical significance :- NA

Coin No. 40

Copper, badly eroded , beyond identification.
Archaeological provenance: *SJN-K 2003, A4, NW, 0.47m, 1, 4301, 1403.*

Coin No. 41

Poor preservation, heavily weathered.
Shape :- Round
Size :- 1.5 cm diameter
Thickness :- 2 mm (0.2 mm)
Weight :- 3.25 gms.
Metal :- Copper or silver alloy

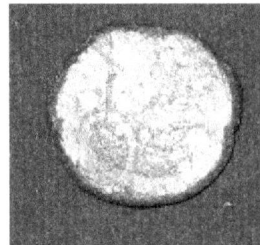

Obv. – Some traces of symbol
Rev. Difficult to identify
Dynasty :- Gadhiya type ?
King :- ----------------------.
Period :- No date on coin,.
Rare : - CCC
Archaeological provenance: *SJN-K 2003, A4, NW, 0.47m, 2, 4207, 1530.*
Historical significance:- NA

Coin No. 42

Shape :- Round
Size :- 1.5 mm diameter
Thickness :- 0.8 mm
Weight :- 0.41 gms.
Metal :- Silver

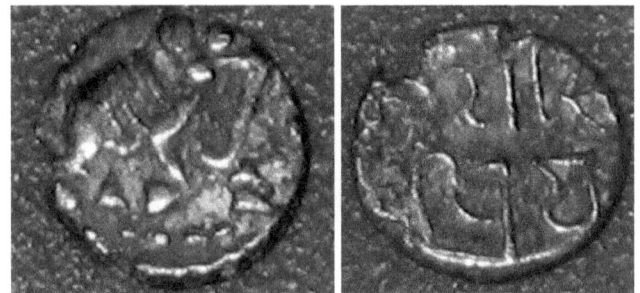

Obverse   Reverse

Obv. Elephant to right with tail in normal position. Dotted border like line below
Rev. Nagari legend reads - *Ja Ya Si [ha] / pi Yah*
Dynasty :- Gujrat Chalukyas
King :- Siddharaj Jaysimha
Period :- No date on coin, 1093 – 1143 A.D.
Rare : - R

Archaeological provenance: *SJN-K 2003, A4, NW,* 0.47m
  (l = 2.50m, b = 1.50m), 2, 4705, 2193.

Historical significance :- Though a known coin , it is in
  good condition . Legend describes: *sri jayasimha priyah.*

Coin No. 43

Shape :- Round
Size :- 1.5 cm diameter
Thickness :- 5 mm
Weight :- 8.70 gms.
Metal :- Copper

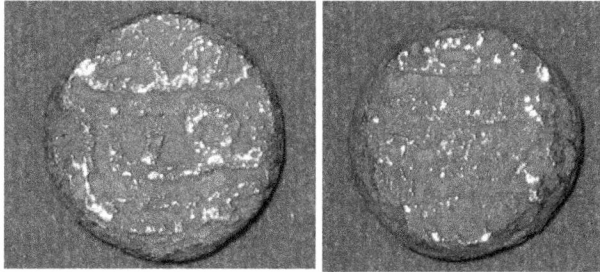

Obverse   Reverse

Obv. Persian Legend, Traces of *al. mustansir ---*
Rev. Persian Legend
Dynasty :- Bahamani Sultan ?
King :- not known
Period :- No date on coin, 1400 – 1500 A.D.
Rare : - CCC
Archaeological provenance: *SJN-K 2003, A5, SW, 0.24m,*
  1, 4901, 1571.
Historical significance :- Nil

Coin No. 44

Shape :- Round
Size :- 1.5 cm diameter
Thickness :- 5 mm
Weight :- 8.70 gms.
Metal :- Copper
Obv. Traces of Arabic Legend,
Rev. Traces of Arabic Legend
Dynasty :- Gujrat Sultan ?
King :- not known
Period :- No date on coin,
Rare : - CCC
Archaeological provenance: *SJN-K 2003, A5, SW, 0.24m,*
  1, 4901, 1570.
Historical significance :- Nil

Coin No. 45

Nickel, badly eroded, beyond identification.
Archaeological provenance: *SJN-K 2003, A5, SW, 0.28m,*
  1, 4902, 1572.
Historical significance :- Nil

Coin No. 46

Copper, badly eroded,
Wt. – 3.69 grams
Archaeological provenance: *SJN-K 2003, A5, SW, 0.28m,*
  1, 4902, 1573.
Historical significance:- Nil

Coin No. 47

Shape :- Round
Size :- 1 mm diameter
Thickness :-
Weight :- 0.14 gms.
Metal :- Silver
Obv. . Symbols
Rev. Plain.
Dynasty :- Early Coin
King :- ------not known------------
Period :- No date on coin,
Rare : - CCC
Archaeological provenance: *SJN-K 2003, A5, SW, 0.44m,*
  2, 4902, 1817.
Historical significance :- Though a known coin, it is one
  of the smallest coins from the excavations. Known as
  MASHAKA coin.

Coin No. 48

Shape :- Round
Size :- 1.5 cm diameter
Thickness :- 2 mm
Weight :- 2.64 gms.
Metal :- Copper

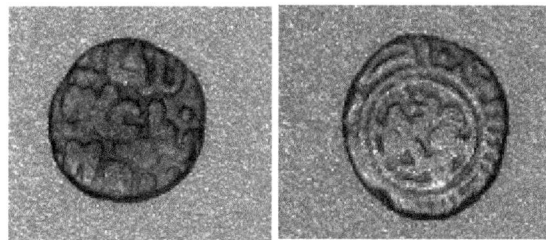

Obverse   Reverse

Obv. Persian legend *al sultan / al aazam ala ud duniya*
Rev. In circle *Muhammad shah* ,
nagari legend encircling *(sultan) 'Alavadin'.*
Dynasty :- Delhi Sultan
King :- Ali Gurshashp , Muhammadsha alias Alauddin
  Khilji.
Period :- No date on coin, 1290- 1320 A.D.
Rare : - CCC
Archaeological provenance: *SJN-K 2003, B3, SW, surface,*
  1283.
Historical significance :- Nil

Coin No. 49

Copper, Coin like object.
Weight :- 2.64 gms.
Archaeological provenance: *SJN-K 2003, B3, SW, ?above feet of HS-2, 2, 1897.*

Coin No. 50

Nickel, modern One rupee coin of Indian Republic.
Archaeological provenance: *SJN-K 2003, B4, SW, 0.12m, 1, 8101, 1684.*

Coin No. 51

Copper, coin like object. No trace of legends.
Archaeological provenance: *SJN-K 2003, B4, NW, 0.20m, 1, 8303, 1767.*

Coin No. 52

Shape :- Round
Size :- 1 cm diameter
Thickness :- 1 mm
Weight :- 0.50 gms.
Metal :- Silver

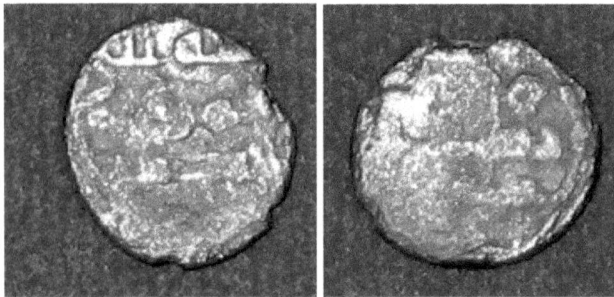

| Obverse | Reverse |

Amir of Sindh: Ruler: Umar ? Arabic legend (but worn out).
Dynasty :- Amirs of Sindh
King :- Amirs of Sindh
Period :- No date on coin, 870 – 1030 A.D.
Rare : - CCC
Archaeological provenance: *SJN-K 2003, B4, NW, 0.28m, 1, 8304, 1784.*

Coin No. 53

Nickel, Modern 25 paisa coin.
Archaeological provenance: *SJN-K 2003, B4, NE, 0.08m, 1, 8501, 1641.*

Coin No. 54

Shape :- Round
Size :- 1.7 cm diameter
Thickness :- 1.5 mm
Weight :- 2.16 gms.
Metal :- Copper

| Obverse | Reverse |

Obv. A seated figure probably of a garuda , two swastika symbols, and one swastika in reverse
Rev. Arabic legends probably *Al sultan or al malik*
Dynasty :- Rashtrakutas ? (identified on the basis of Garuda Mudra on the Rashtrakuta copper plates)
King :- ---------not known----------------
Period :- No date on coin, 700 – 900 A.D.
Rare : - RRR
Archaeological provenance: *SJN-K 2003, B4, NE, 0.18m, 1, 8503, 1655.*
Historical significance :- First Known coins of this type, extremely rare, unique human or anthropomorphic figure of Garuda with swastika and Arabic legend.

Similar type of coins were also issued by the Arab Governors of Sind, (712 – 870 ACE), with six pointed stars within geometric pattern formed by two overlapping squares on one side and the name of the governor on other (Goron and Goenka 2001: xxii).

Coin No. 55

Shape :- Round
Size :- 1.4 cm diameter
Thickness :- 2 mm (0.2 cm)
Weight :- 3.44 gms.
Metal :- Alloy base silver

Obv. Crude face of a king
Rev. Iranian fire alter
Dynasty :- Gadhiya type
King :- --------not known-------------
Period :- No date on coin, 6th century onwards.
Rare : - CCC
Archaeological provenance: *SJN-K 2003, B5, SE, 0.11m, 1, 9501, 1625.*
Historical significance :- NA

Coin No. 56

Shape :- Round
Size :- 1.5 cm diameter
Thickness :- 2 mm
Weight :- 3.87 gms.
Metal :- Copper

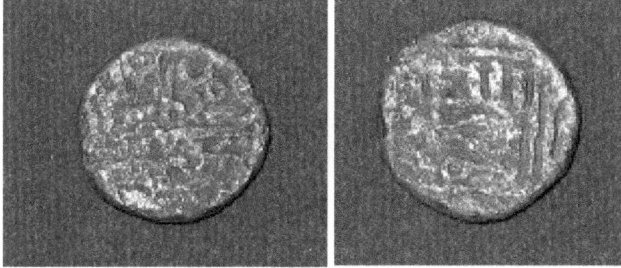

Gujarat sultanate: Ruler : Ahmad Shah I (AD 1411-1442)
Obv. Arabic legend, but worn out.
Rev. Ahmad shah as-sultan within square.
Dynasty :- Gujrat Sultan
King :- Ahmad Shah I (AD 1411-1442)
Period :- No date on coin,
Rare : - CCC
Archaeological provenance: *SJN-K 2003, B5, SE, 0.11m, 1, 9501, 1626.*
Historical significance :- Nil

Coin No. 57

Shape :- Irregular Round
Size :- 1.3 cm diameter
Thickness :- 2 mm
Weight :- 2.11 gms.
Metal :- Copper may be plated with silver

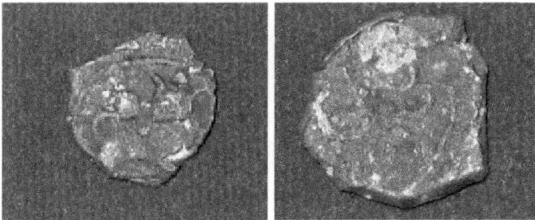

Obverse   Reverse

Obv. Lion to right with tail upraised. Dotted border like line below
Rev. Late Brahmi legends, reads - *Shri ....*
Dynasty :- Gujrat Chalukyas ?
King :- ----------not known----------------
Period :- No date on coin, 700-900 A.D.
Rare : - RRR
Archaeological provenance: *SJN-K 2003, B5, SW, 0.13m, 1, 89011616.*
Historical significance :- A known, earlier reported coin , but a rare type. This type of lion figure is seen on the coins of Seunachandra II of the Yadavas of Devagiri.

Coin No. 58

Shape :- Round
Size :- 1.7 cm diameter
Thickness :- 7 mm
Weight :- 13.36 gms.
Metal :- Copper
Obv. – Some traces of Arabic legends.
May be a Gujrat Sultan Coin.
Archaeological provenance: *SJN-K 2003, B5, SW, 0.13m, 1, 8901, 1617.*

Coin No. 59

Copper, coin- like object. No trace of any legends.
Archaeological provenance: *SJN-K 2003, B5, SW, 0.26m, 1,8903, 1856.*

Coin No. 60

Shape :- Round
Size :- 9 mm diameter
Thickness :- 0.1 mm
Weight :- 0.37 gms.
Metal :- Silver

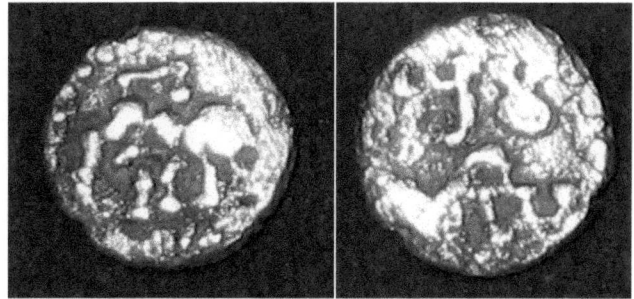

Obv. Elephant with rider to left.
Rev. Brahmi legends reads - *Aa Ma ... (va) sa*
Dynasty :- Rashtrakuta
King :- Amoghavarsha ?
Period :- No date on coin, 700 -900 A.D.
Rare : - RRR
Archaeological provenance: *SJN-B 2004, surface, 3430.*
Historical significance :- First Known coins of this type, extreme rare.

Coin No. 61

Shape :- Round
Size :- 1.5 cm diameter
Thickness :- 2 mm (0.2 cm)
Weight :- 3.11 gms.
Metal :- Silver mixed Billon

Arabic legend:
 Obv. *as-sultan al-ghazi ghiyas-ud-duniya waddin*
 Rev. *Abul muzaffar Tughlaq shah*
Dynasty :- Delhi Sultan , Tughlaq
King :- Giyasuddin Tughlaq
Period :- Traces of date on coin, (725 -752 AH) 1320 – 1325 A.D.
Rare : - CCC
Archaeological provenance: *SJN-B 2004, surface, 2465.*
Historical significance :- NA

Coin No. 62

Shape :- Round
Size :- 1.7 cm diameter
Thickness :- 1 MM
Weight :- 2.01 gms.
Metal :- Copper

Obverse   Reverse

Obv. A seated figure probably of a garuda, two swastika symbols, one is a reverse swastik
Rev. Arabic legends probably *Al sultan or al malik*
Dynasty :- Rashtrakutas ? (on the basis of Garuda Mudra on Rashtrakuta copper plates.)
King :- ---------not known ----------------
Period :- No date on coin, 700 – 900 A.D.
Rare : - RRR
Archaeological provenance: *SJN-B 2004, TT4, NE, 0.64m, 2, 51516, 2967.*
Historical significance :- First Known coins of this type, extreme rare, unique human or anthropomorphic figure of Garuda with swastika and Arabic legend, that makes it a unique in character.

Similar type of coins were also issued by the Arab Governors of Sind, (712 – 870 ACE), six pointed star within geometric pattern formed by two overlapping squares on one side and the name of the governor on other (Goron and Goenka 2001: xxii).

Coin No. 63

Shape :- Round
Size :- 1.3 cm diameter
Thickness :- 2 mm
Weight :- 2.01 gms.
Metal :- Copper

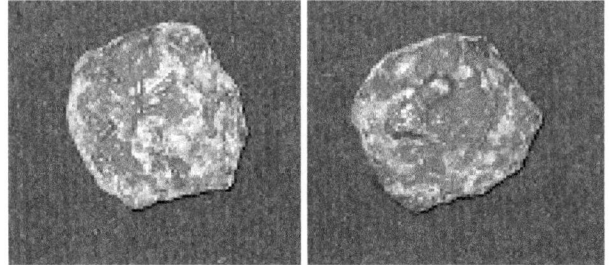

Obverse   Reverse

Obv. A star like figure
Rev. Traces of an unidentifiable animal figure
Dynasty Chalukya type
King :- ---------not known----------------
Period :- No date on coin, 700 – 900 A.D.
Rare : - RRR
Archaeological provenance: *SJN-B 2004, TT4, NE, 0.85m, 2, 51522, 3023.*
Historical significance :- NA

Coin No. 64

Shape :- Round
Size :- 8 mm diameter
Thickness :- 1 MM
Weight :- 0.64 gms.
Metal :- Copper

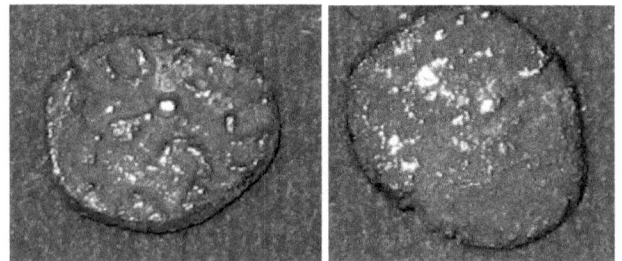

Obv. Late Brahmi legend *Shri ra ja ... .*
Rev. eroded
Dynasty :- Uncertain
King :- --------not known-----------
Period :- No date on coin, 700 – 900 A.D.
Rare : - RRR
Archaeological provenance: *SJN-B 2004, TT4, NE, 1.96m, 5, 51549, 3287.*
Historical significance :- rare type issued on Kalchuri Krishnaraja type.

Coin No. 65

Copper, coin-like object. Piece of copper. No trace of legends.
Archaeological provenance: *SJN-B 2004, TT4, NE, 2.76m, 5, 51565, 3383.*

Coin No. 66

Shape :- generally Round
Size :- 1.5 * 1.2 cm diameter
Thickness :-
Weight :- 2.32 gms.
Metal :- Copper

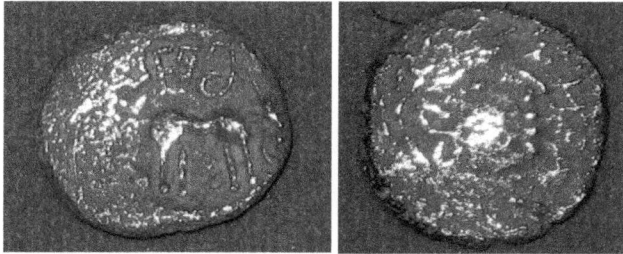

Obv. Elephant to right with tail in normal position. Dotted border like line below, Brahmi legends – *Shri ... Ja Shri...*
Rev. Portrait of a king to right
Dynasty :- Gujrat Chalukyas ? Kalchuri type coin, hitherto unique.
King :- ----? ------
Period :- No date on coin, 600-800 A.D. on paleographic grounds
Rare : - RRR
Archaeological provenance: *SJN-B 2004, TT4, NE, 3.09m, 6, 51573, 3399.*
Historical significance :- Unpublished coin , it is in good condition. Nicely executed portrait. The script on the coin resembles with the coin of Jayāśraya (Mirashi 1962 : 118-120.)

Coin No. 67

Copper, Effaced.
Archaeological provenance: *SJN-B 2004, TT4, NW, 3.51, 6, 51581, 3410.*

Coin No. 68

Shape :- generally Round
Size :- 1 cm diameter
Thickness :- 1mm
Weight :- 0.46 gms.
Metal :- Copper
Obv. Traces of Brahmi legends – *pa na...*
Rev.
Dynasty :- . indeterminate.
King :- not known
Period :- No date on coin, Post 6th century A.D.
Rare : - RRR

Archaeological provenance: *SJN-B 2004, TT4, NW, 0.75m, 2, 51320, 3047.*
Historical significance :- nil.

Coin No. 69

Shape :- Round
Size :- 1.2 cm diameter
Thickness :- 2 mm
Weight :- 1.55 gms.
Metal :- Silver

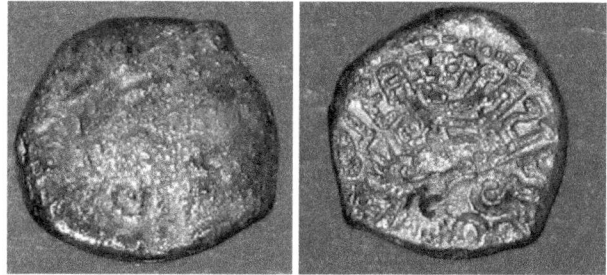

Obverse   Reverse

Obv. Portrait of a King
Rev. Brahmi legends - figure of a peacock Brahmi legend around ... *Maha Raja Shri Kumargupta ....*
Dynasty :- Gupta
King – Kumargupta I
Period :- 415-455 A.D.
Rare : - CCC
Archaeological provenance: *SJN-B 2004, TT4, NW, 0.92m, 3, 51327, 3089.*
Historical significance :- Gujrat issues of Kumar Gupta I.

Coin No. 70

Shape :- Round
Size :- 1.7 cm diameter
Thickness :- 4 mm (0.4 cm)
Weight :- 8.56 gms.
Metal :- Copper

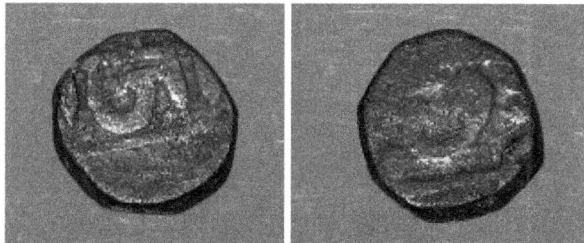

Obverse   Reverse

Obv. Devanagari legend – *(Sri) / ra ja*
Rev. *chh tra / { pa ti}.*
Dynasty :- Marathas, Peshwa period.
King :- Peshwa period.
Period :- No date on coin, 1700-1800 A.D..
Rare : - CCC

Archaeological provenance: *SJN-B 2004, TT4, SW, 0.32m, 2, 51105, 2771.*
Historical significance :- Maratha coin. Shivarai

Coin No. 71

Shape :- Round
Size :- 1.4 cm diameter
Thickness :- 0.5 mm
Weight :- 1.01 gms.
Metal :- Copper

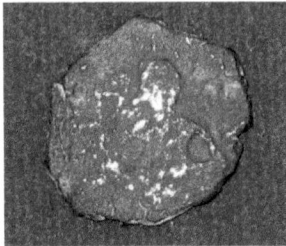

Obverse

Obv. A seated figure probably a garuda , two swastika symbols , one reverse swastika.
Rev. Arabic legends probably *Al sultan or al malik.*
Dynasty :- Rashtrakutas ? (on the basis of Garuda Mudra on Rashtrakuta copper plates.)
King :- ---------?----------------
Period :- No date on coin, 700 – 900 A.D.
Rare : - RRR
Archaeological provenance: *SJN-B 2004, TT4, SW, 0.32m, 2, 51105, 2771.*
Historical significance :- First Known coins of this type, extreme rare, unique human or anthropomorphic figure of Garuda with swastika and Arabic legend

Similar type of coins were also issued by the Arab Governors of Sind, (712 – 870 A.D.), six pointed star within geometric pattern formed by two overlapping squares on one side and the name of the governor on other. (Goron and Goenka 2001: xxii).

Coin No. 72

Shape :- Round
Size :- 1.1 cm diameter
Thickness :- 2 mm
Weight :- 2.05 gms.
Metal :- Copper

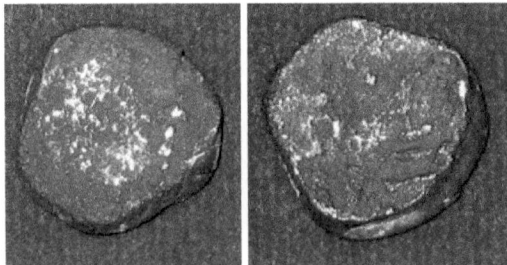

Obverse   Reverse

Obv. Portrait
Rev. Traces of Post Gupta Brahmi legend.
Dynasty :- ?
King :- --------not known---------------
Period :- No date on coin, 700 – 900 A.D.
Rare : - RRR
Archaeological provenance: *SJN-B 2004, TT4, SW, 3.67m, 2 (well deposit), 51140, 3318.*
Historical significance :- First Known coins of this type.

Coin No. 73

Nickel, Modern 25 Paisa coin of Indian republic.
Archaeological provenance: *SJN-D 2004, ?, 1.15m, 1, ?, 2361.*

Coin No. 74

Copper, No legends.
Archaeological provenance: *SJN-D 2004, L1, NW, 1.42m, 1, 14508, 2548.*

Coin No. 75

Shape :- Round small
Size :- 1.2 cm diameter
Thickness :- 0.5 mm (0.05 cm)
Weight :- 0.39 gms.
Metal :- Silver

Obverse   Reverse

Amir Of Sindh ;
Ruler (Amir):Umar (period 9thcentury AD)
Obv. In kufic Kufic calligraphy; *Allah yasiq umar wa fansar*
Rev. In Kufic calligraphy *Allah Muhammad rasul allah Umar*.
Dynasty :- Amirs of Sindh 870 – 1030 A.D.
King :- Umar
Period :- No date on coin, 870 – 1030 A.D.
Rare : - R
Archaeological provenance: *SJN-D 2004, L2, SW, 0.42m, 1, 15204, 2547.*
Historical significance :- Coin of Amirs of Sindh

Coin No. 76

Shape :- Round small
Size :- 0.9 cm diameter
Thickness :- 1 mm (0.1 cm)

Weight :- 0.86 gms.
Metal :- Silver

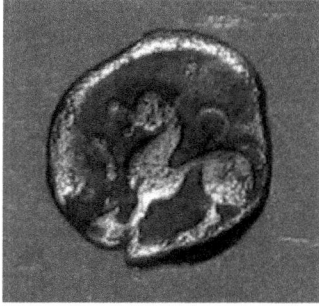

Obverse

Obv. Lion or Vyala to left with tail upraised, forepaw
  upraised.
Rev. Traces of devanagari legend.
Dynasty :- Yadavas of Devagiri

King :- Singhana
Period :- No date on coin, 1250-1270 A.D.
Rare : - R
Archaeological provenance: *SJN-D 2004, MX1, NE, 1.16m,*
  1, 24301, 2442.
Historical significance :- Coin of Yadavas of Devagiri.

Coin No. 77

Nickel, Modern coin of Indian Republic of 1984 A.D.
Archaeological provenance: *SJN-D 2004, OX1, NE, 1.07m,*
  1, 34501, 2640.

Coin No. 78

Copper, Effaced, No legends.
Archaeological provenance: *SJN-D 2004, OX1, NE, 1.28m,*
  2, 31708, 2690.

Checklist of Coins from Excavations at Sanjan

SL.NO	LOCATION	TRENCH	DEPTH	LAYER	LOT	REG.NO.	METAL
1	SJN-B 2002	TT1, NE	Surface	-	-	11	silver / lead
2	SJN-B 2002	-	Surface	-	-	1119	Copper
3	SJN-B 2002	-	Surface	-	-	1118	Copper
4	SJN-B 2002	TT1, SW	0.40m	1	102	160	Silver (label = silver / Copper)
5	SJN-B 2002	TT1, SW	0.40m (l = 0.70m, b = 2m)	1	102	161	Silver
6	SJN-B 2002	TT1, SW	1.59m	3	140	1060	Copper
7	SJN-B 2002	TT1, SW	1.16m (outside pit)	3	137	1045	Copper
8	SJN-B 2002	TT1, SE	0.63m	2	707	80	Copper
9	SJN-B 2002	TT1, SE	1.79m	3	715	1134	Copper
10	SJN-B 2002	TT1, NE	0.46m	1	502	45	Silver
11	SJN-B 2002	TT1, NE	0.57m	1	503	68	Copper
12*	SJN-B 2004	-	Surface	-	-	2350	Copper
13	SJN-B 2002	TT1, NE	0.71m	2	504	103	Copper
14	SJN-B 2002	TT1, NE	1.04m (l = 3.20m, b = 3.32m)	3	512	243	Silver
15	SJN-B 2002	TT1, NE	1.04m (l = 3.80m, b = 3.14m)	3	512	242	Silver
16	SJN-B 2002	TT1, NE	1.24m	3	517	980	Silver
17	SJN-B 2002	TT1, NW	Not given	Not given	Not given	13	Copper
18	SJN-B 2002	TT1, NW	1.07m	3	318	738	Copper
19	SJN-B 2002	TT1, NW	1.18m	3	321	800	Copper
20	SJN-B 2002	TT2, SW	0.66m	1	903	335	Copper
21	SJN-B 2002	TT2, SW	0.74m	2	905	343	Copper
22	SJN-B 2002	TT2, SW	0.74m	2	905	344	Labelled as lead
23	SJN-B 2002	TT2, SW	1.17m	3	913	389	Silver
24	SJN-B 2002	TT2, SE	0.81m	2	1509	401	Copper
25	SJN-B 2002	TT2, SE	0.81m	2	1509	399	Copper
26	SJN-B 2002	TT2, SE	1.52m	3	1522	662	Lead
27	SJN-B 2002	TT2, SE	1.52m	3	1522	563	Copper (label says copper with silver coating)
28	SJN-B 2002	TT2, SE	1.67m	4	1525	607	Silver? (label says copper)
29	SJN-B 2002	TT2, SE	2.01m	4	1532	688	Copper
30	SJN-K 2003	Surface	From back-filling	-	-	2312	Copperr
31	SJN-K 2003	Surface	-	-	-	2311	?
32	SJN-K 2003	Surface	-	-	-	2330	Copper
33	SJN-K 2003	Surface	-	-	-	2143	Silver
34	SJN-K 2003	Surface	-	-	-	2119	Copper
35	SJN-K 2003	Surface	-	-	-	1813	Copper
36	SJN-K 2003	A3, SE	0.30m	1	3901	1196	?
37	SJN-K 2003	A3, SE	0.74m	3	3909	1258	Copper
38	SJN-K 2003	A4, SW	0.18m	1	4101	1355	Copper
39	SJN-K 2003	A4, SW	0.18m	1	4101	1350	Copper
40	SJN-K 2003	A4, NW	0.19m	1	4301	1403	Copper
41	SJN-K 2003	A4, NW	0.47m	2	4307	1530	Silver (label says copper)
42	SJN-K 2003	A4, NW	0.47m (l = 2.50m, b = 1.50m)	2	4705 (this lot no does not tally with tr. & quad series)	2193	Silver

SL.NO	LOCATION	TRENCH	DEPTH	LAYER	LOT	REG.NO.	METAL
43	SJN-K 2003	A5, SW	0.24m	1	4901	1571	Copper
44	SJN-K 2003	A5, SW	0.24m	1	4901	1570	Copper
45	SJN-K 2003	A5, SW	0.28m	1	4902	1572	Label says 'Iron'
46	SJN-K 2003	A5, SW	0.28m	1	4902	1573	Copper
47	SJN-K 2003	A5, SW	0.44m	2	4906	1817	Silver
48	SJN-K 2003	B3, SW	Surface	-	-	1283	Copper
49	SJN-K 2003	B3, SW	? (above feet of HS-2)	2	-	1897	Copper
50	SJN-K 2003	B4, SW	0.12m	1	8101	1684	Copper
51	SJN-K 2003	B4, NW	0.20m	1	8303	1767	Copper
52	SJN-K 2003	B4, NW	0.28m	1	8304	1784	Silver? Copper?
53	SJN-K 2003	B4, NE	0.08m	1	8501	1641	?
54	SJN-K 2003	B4, NE	0.18m	1	8503	1655	Copper?
55	SJN-K 2003	B5, SE	0.11m	1	9501	1625	Silver
56	SJN-K 2003	B5, SE	0.11m	1	9501	1626	Copper
57	SJN-K 2003	B5, SW	0.13m	1	8901	1616	Silver
58	SJN-K 2003	B5, SW	0.13m	1	8901	1617	Copper
59	SJN-K 2003	B5, SW	0.26m	1	8903	1856	Copper
60	SJN-B 2004	Surface	-	-	-	3430	Silver
61	SJN-B 2004	Surface	-	-	-	2465	Silver
62	SJN-B 2004	TT4, NE	0.64m	2	51516	2967	Copper
63	SJN-B 2004	TT4, NE	0.85m	2	51522	3023	Copper
64	SJN-B 2004	TT4, NE	1.96m	5	51549	3287	Copper
65	SJN-B 2004	TT4, NE	2.76m	5	51565	3383	Copper
66	SJN-B 2004	TT4, NE	3.09m	6	51573	3399	Copper
67	SJN-B 2004	TT4, NE	3.51m	6	51581	3410	Copper
68	SJN-B 2004	TT4, NW	0.75m	2	51320	3047	Silver?
69	SJN-B 2004	TT4, NW	0.92m	3	51327	3089	Silver
70	SJN-B 2004	TT4, SW	0.32m	2	51105	2771	Copper
71	SJN-B 2004	TT4, SW	0.58m	2 (well deposit)	51114	2952	Copper
72	SJN-B 2004	TT4, SW	3.67m	2 (well deposit)	51140	3318	Copper
73	SJN-D 2004	?	1.15m	1	?	2361	?
74	SJN-D 2004	L1, NW	1.42m	1	14508	2548	Copper
75	SJN-D 2004	L2, SW	0.42m	1	15204	2547	Silver
76	SJN-D 2004	MX1, NE	1.16m	1	24301	2442	Silver
77	SJN-D 2004	OX1, NE	1.07m	1	34501	2640	Aluminium
78	SJN-D 2004	OX1, NE	1.28m	2	31708	2690	Copper

Comparative Chart showing the chronology of Sanjan based upon epigraphs, coins, texts

Sr. No.	Epigraphs mentioning Sanjān	Period AD	Coins found in excavations at Sanjān (2002 – 2004) Ruler – Dynasty Coin No.	No. of coins found	Period A.D.	Literary Evidence
01	Nagarjunakonda Inscription of Abhira Vasushena *(Sanjayapuri)*	278-279	------	-----	3rd	Ibn Khurdādabāh (Arab Traveler) Refers – *Sandān*.*
02	------------	-------	Kumar Gupta 69	01	415-425	-------
03	------------	--------	Uncertain/ Trikutaka Kalchuri type 16,23,	02	500 – 600	--------
04	CP of Chalukya Buddhavarsha Governor of North Konkan , Cousin Brother of Pulakeshi II	611–643	Uncertain/ Kalchuri/ Chalukya type 63,64,66	03	600-700	--------
05	Sanjan CP of Rashtrakuta Amoghvarsha I	793-871	Gadhiya 4,5,10,19, 27, 28,41,55	08	600-900	--------
06	Chinchni CP of Rashtrakuta Indra III Ref .of Sanjan Given to Madhumati by Krishna II	926	Iranian 14	01	700-900 ?	--------
07	Chinchni CP of Rashtrakuta Krishna III	10th CE	Rashtrakuta 15,60	02	700-900	--------
08	--------	--------	Rashtrakuta /Arab Gov. 11,25,54, 62,71	05	700-900/ 712 -870.	--------
09	Janjira CP of Aparajit shilahara Ref. defeat of Arab Feudatories	993	Arab Governors of Sind / Amirs of Sind 8.	01	712-870/ 870-1030	--------
10	Chinchni CP of Chamundaraj feudatory of Shilahara Chhitaraj	1034	Amirs of Sind 7,33,52,75,	04	870-1030	--------
11	Chinchni CP of Modha ruler Vijjaldeva Mahamandaleshwar of Shilahara	1048	--------	----- ---	--------	Al Beruni – Tarikh e Hind Mentions *Sandān*
12	Chinchni CP of Modha ruler Vijjaldeva Mahamandaleshwar of Shilahara	1053	Gujarat Chalukyas Siddharaj Jaysinha 42	01	1093-1143	--------
13	Defeat of Modha rulers by Shilahara Mummuni (Thane Shilahara)	1053 -1070	--------	----- ---	--------	--------
14	--------	--------	Yadavas of Devagiri 76	01	1250-1270	--------
15	--------	--------	Delhi Sultans 1,3,30,34, 48,61	06	1266-1556	--------
16	--------	--------	Gujrat Sultan 44,56, 58	03	1403-1553	--------
17	--------	--------	Bahamani ? 43	01	1400-1500	--------
18	--------	--------	Maratha (Later Shivarai) 12,17, 70,	03	1700-1800	Dastur Boman Kaikobād
19	--------	--------	British India and Indian Republic	07	1857-2000	--------

* Motichandra 2010: 254-55.

Gadheya type coins at Sanjan excavations:

Catalogue no.	Regis. no	Location	Trench	Depth	Layer	Metal	Size	Thickness	weight
4	160	SJN-B 2002	TT1, SW	0.40m	1	Alloy base silver	1.5cm	2.5mm	3.19gms
5	161	SJN-B 2002	TT1, SW	0.40m (I =0.70m, b= 2m)	1	Alloy base silver	1.5cm	2.5mm	3.29gms
10	45	SJN-B 2002	TT1, NE	0.46m	1	Alloy base silver	1.5cm	4.00mm	3.39gms
19	800	SJN-B 2002	TT1, NW	1.18m	3	Alloy base silver	1.5cm	4.00mm	4.04gms
27	563	SJN-B 2002	TT2, SE	1.52m	3	Alloy base silver	1.5cm	2.00mm	3.64gms
28	607	SJN-B 2002	TT2, SE	1.67m	4	Alloy base silver	1.6cm	2.00mm	3.61gms
41	1530	SJN-K 2003	A4,NW	0.47m (1 = 2.50mb = 1.50m)	2	Copper or billion	1.5cm	2.00mm	3.25gms
55	1625	SJN-K 2003	B5, SE	0.11m	1	Alloy base silver	1.4cm	2.00mm	3.44gms

Coins of British India, Indian Republic and unidentifiable, effaced coins and/or coin like objects from Sanjan excavations:

Catalogue no.	Regis. no	Location	Trench	Depth	Layer	Metal	Remarks
2	1119	SJN-B 2002	--	Surface	---	Copper	British India 1915, ½ anna, eroded, effaced
13	103	SJN-B 2002	TT1, NE	0.71m	2	Copper	Completely eroded, effaced
18	738	SJN-B 2002	TT1, NW	1.07m	3	Copper	Totally eroded, coin-like object
20	335	SJN-B 2002	TT2, SW	0.66m	1	Copper	Effaced, beyond identification
21	343	SJN-B 2002	TT2, SW	0.74m	2	Copper	0.36gms, completely eroded
22	344	SJN-B 2002	TT2, SW	0.74m	2	Lead	Broken and twisted fragment, completely eroded, 0.36gms weight, probably not a coin
24	401	SJN-B 2002	TT2, SE	0.81m	2	Copper	unidentifiable
26	662	SJN-B 2002	TT2, SE	1.52cm	3	Lead	Not a coin, coin-like object
31	2311	SJN-K 2003	Surface	--	--	Copper	British India, ½ anna coin of George VI, 1946
132	2330	SJN-K 2003	Surface	--	--	Copper	May be a coin, effaced.
35	1813	SJN-K 2003	Surface	--	--	Copper	Totally eroded, effaced
36	1196	SJN-K 2003	A3, SE	0.30m	1	Copper	British India, ½ anna coin of George VI, 1946
37	1258	SJN-K 2003	A3, SE	0.74m	3	Copper	Completely eroded
14	1355	SJN-K 2003	A4, SW	0.18m	1	Copper	Effaced, unidentifiable
40	1403	SJN-K 2003	A4, NW	0.19m	1	Copper	Effaced, unidentifiable
45	1572	SJN-K 2003	A5, SW	0.28m	1	Iron	Badly eroded, beyond identification
46	1573	SJN-K 2003	A5, SW	0.28m	1	Copper	Badly eroded, 3.69gms weight
49	1897	SJN-K 2003	B3, SW	?(above feet of HS-2)	2	Copper	Coin –like object, 2.64 gms
50	1684	SJN-K 2003	B4, SW	0.12m	1	Nickel	Modern one rupee denomination of Indian Republic
51	1767	SJN-K 2003	B4, SW	0.20m	1	Copper	Coin –like object
53	1641	SJN-K 2003	B4, NE	0.08m	1	Nickel	25 paise coin of Indian Republic
59	1856	SJN-K 2003	B4, SW	0.26m	1	Copper	Coin –like object, no trace of legends
65	3383	SJN-K 2003	TT4, NE	2.76m	5	Copper	Piece of copper, coin-like object with no trace of legends

Catalogue no.	Regis. no	Location	Trench	Depth	Layer	Metal	Remarks
67	3410	SJN-B 2004	TT4, NE	3.51m	6	Copper	Effaced
73	2361	SJN-D 2004	?	1.15m	1	Nickel	25 paise coin of Indian Republic of 1986
74	2548	SJN-D 2004	L1, NW	1.42m	1	Copper	Copper, no legends
77	2640	SJN-D 2004	OX1, NE	1.07m	1	Aluminium	20 paise coin of Indian Republic, 1984
78	2690	SJN-D 2004	OX1, NE	1.28m	2	Copper	Small, eroded, effaced, no legends visible.

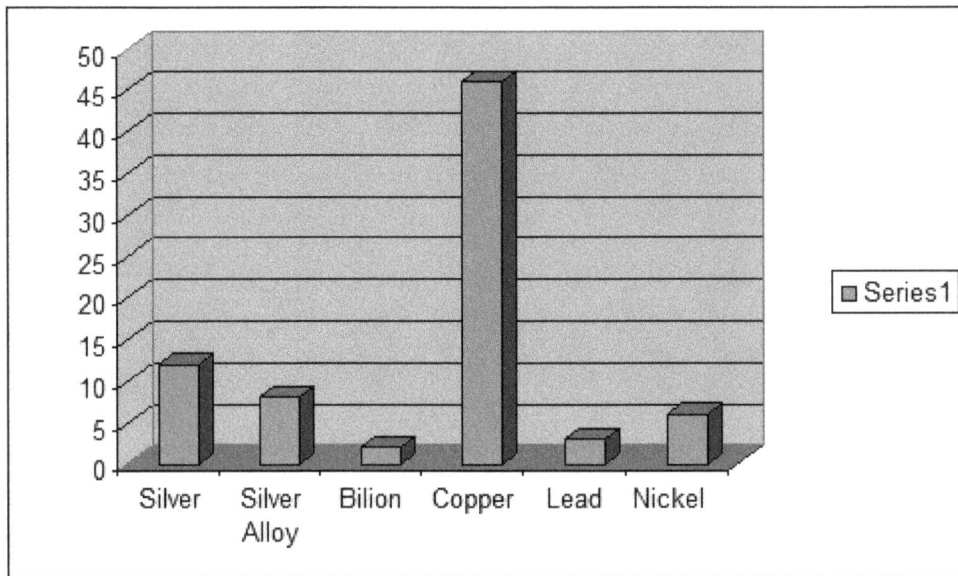

Metal-wise representation of coins at Sanjan.

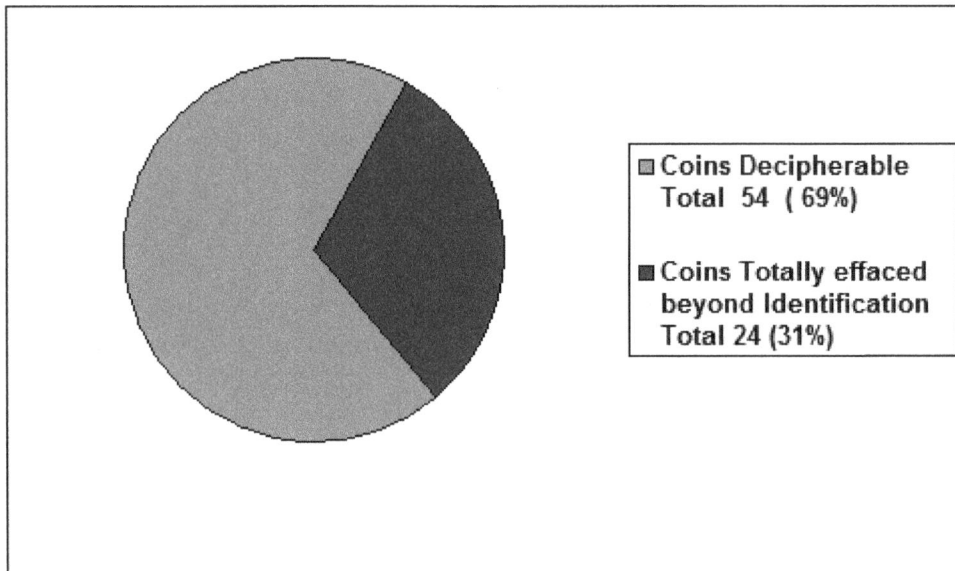

Ratio of decipherable and effaced coins at Sanjan.

Discussion and conclusions

The excavations in the years 2002, 2003, 2004 have yielded 29, 30, 19 number of coins respectively. Out of the total of 78 coins, 13 coins are surface finds. Among the 13 coins, except the coin No. 60, all others pertain to Medieval and Modern periods of History.

Due to weathering and inherent coastal humid conditions the majority of the coins from excavations are effaced and corroded. Often the authors were confronted with difficulties of ascertaining the coins to a precise date and the exact identification of a particular ruler. As a result only 69% coins out of the total assemblage could be studied conclusively. Metal-wise analysis shows majority of them on copper, followed by silver and alloy on silver and there is a definite grain of consistency with the type of coin and the metal. However, integrating other associational evidence such as of stratigraphy, symbols, paleography, metrology, weight of coins, general fabric and also with the ancillary help of Numismatic Geography, it has become possible to classify the coins in broad series and assign a chronological frame of time. A total of 54 i.e. 69% coins are in decipherable condition and they definitely provide an interesting picture of the economic activities at Sanjan and adjoining territories.

The very absence of any Punch marked , Satvahana, Kshatrapa and even early Kalchuri coins in the assemblage, the fact corroborated by epigraphical sources and stratigraphy of the present site, suggest that Sanjan and 'Samyana Mandal' was at its zenith during the Rashtrakuta period (700 – 900 A. D).

As far as the coin is concerned, the continuous numismatic chronology at Sanjan spans only between the 5th century A.D. to 13th Century A.D. No coins having clear symbols or paleography or with the legends which identifies the ruler, prior to the 5th century are evident at Sanjan excavations.

Gadhiya and Garuda type of Coins

If the monetary functioning of this place or area is to be studied at all, it should rely on the presence of a relatively large no of coins. In this respect Gadhiya , Garuda / Arabic legend type of coins are comparatively more in number (see table on Gadheya coins), and they are useful in strengthening the premise based on the epigraphic evidence that Sanjan was a flourishing centre from the 6th century CE to 9th century CE. This is further supported by the Numismatic Geography of Sanjan (http://www. asiaurangabad.in/index/epigraphical_and_numismatical. aspx). Indo-Sassanian coins or Gadhiya coins are commonly found in Konkan and Saurashtra and can be assigned a time frame of 6th to 11th century AD.

Rashtrakuta Coins:

The sterling numismatic discoveries at the site of Sanjan are

the inscribed coins (No. 15 & 60), attributed to Rashtrakuta ruler Amoghavarsha I (793 – 871 ACE.). Similarly, some coin types have been brought to light for the first time by Sanjan excavations (coin nos. 16, 29, 64, 66, 72). The further research on these well preserved coins may help in identifying actual ruler who issued them and may help in understanding better the coinage of Rashtrakutas in particular with special reference to the political jurisdiction of Sanjan.

Coins of the Amirs of Sind

It is also noteworthy that the coins of the Arab Governors of Sind and the Amirs of Sind are present in a good number from excavations. These coins were concurrent in present Gujrat and North Konkan is no exception to Sanjan.

Swastika – Anthropomorphic Garuda / Arabic legend type coins

A unique feature of the coins unearthed at Sanjan is the discovery of an yet enigmatic type i.e. Swastika – Anthropomorphic Garuda / Arabic legends. There are a total of 5 (nos. 11, 25, 54, 62, 71.) coins have been reported, it is worth noting that these coins are observed generally in association with the Gadhiya type of coins. Historical significance of these coins is appreciated by being the first of its type, extremely rare, bearing unique human or anthropomorphic figure of Garuda with swastika and Arabic legend. Similar type of coins was also issued by the Arab Governors of Sind, (712 – 870 A.D.). Goron and Goenka (2001: xxii) have shown the evidence of similar type having six pointed stars within geometric pattern formed by two overlapping squares on one side and the name of the governor on other.

Coins of Gujrat Chalukya and Yadava

The silver coin of Gujrat Chalukya Siddharaj Jaysinha and the silver piece of Yadavas of Devagiri are also important regarding the territorial expansion of the respective dynasties.

Coins of Delhi Sultans and Gujrat Sultans

The common type of coins of Delhi sultanate is also reported here, as has been reported commonly in other parts of Maharashtra. The hordes of these coins are most profusely found in the Deccan and its common presence in the region does not warrant any specific description.

Foreign Coin type

Coin no. 14 (Abbasid- Iranian) is from Iran, though it is a small broken piece with Kufic, it is an indicative of the maritime trade of that time.

Concluding Remarks

Coins bearing statigraphic control such as at Sanjan emerge as an important and indispensible numismatic evidence of economic conditions prevailing in and around Sanjan throughout the thousand year's history of the site. The numismatic data when integrated with epigraphic and literary record, a clear picture of events in chronological order emerge as a supportive piece of evidence. The preservation of coins is generally poor and hence several of them have been deprived of precise identification. Being in close proximity to the river, periodic floods and subsequent erosion has led to disturbance of the site and hence many of the coins (especially those of British India and Indian Republic) are sometimes coming from lower levels, indicating intrusion of recent materials. This is specially seen in the context of the finds from TT1 while the TT4 with respect to thirteen coins, mostly belonging to the period between 7th to 9th C A.D. provide a definite time frame for this part of habitation. The sole coin of Kumargupta I offers the possibilities of either its prolonged tenure of circulation or an early date of 5th century for the initial chronological base for the Sanjan numismatic assemblage. As regards the coins from *Dokhma* (Tower of silence), out of a total of six coins, only two of them could be identified as belonging to Amirs of Sind and Yadavas respectively. Rashtrakuta coins are a perpetual rarity and besides only the two known coins issued by the king Karkaraja and Dhruv, the two new ones assigned to Amoghvarsha I are one of the most important and welcome discoveries coming to light with reference to Rashtrakutas. Sporadic occurrence of Gujarat Chalukyas and Yadavas however limit any further comments.

Acknowledgements

Authors are grateful to Dr. Homi Dhalla, President World Zarathushti Cultural Foundation (WZCF), Mumbai for entrusting the coins for study. Thanks are due to late Dr. S.P. Gupta, and the excavation team. Dr. Shailendra Bhandare of Ashmolean Museum, Oxford, U.K. offered valuable suggestions in identifying the coins of Amoghavarsha I, for which authors are thankful to him. The suggestions and corrections in identification of some of the coins by Dr. Danish Moin of the Indian Institute of Research in Numismatic Studies, Anjneri, Nasik are gratefully acknowledged.

References

Bhandare S.U. 2000. A Copper coin of Rashrtakuta Dhruva , in *IIRNS NEWSLINE,* issue 27 (Amiteshwar Jha Ed.), p.4. Nasik –Anjaneri.

Gokhale Shobhana . 2004. Coins found in the Excavations at Sanjan – 2002 , in *Journal of Indian Ocean Archaeology,* No. 1, pp. 107-112.

Goron Stan., J.P Goenka. 2001. *The Coins OF THE Indian Sultanates*, Munshiram Manoharlal Publications.

Gupta, S.P. , Dalal K, Dandekar, A., Nanji, R Mitra R. And R, Pandey 2002. A Preliminary Report on the Excavations at Sanjan (2002). *Purattatva* 32: 182-198.

Gupta, S.P. , Dalal K, Dandekar, A., Nanji, R, Pandey R and R. Mitra 2003. Early medieval Indian Ocean Trade: Excavations at Sanjan, India. *Circle of Inner Asian Art Newsletter 17*: 26-34.

Gupta, S.P. , Dalal K, Dandekar, A., Nanji, R, Arvazhi P., and Bomble, S. 2004. On the footsteps of the Zoroastrian Parsis in India: Excavations at Sanjan on the West Coast- 2003. *Journal of Indian Ocean Archaeology 1*: 93-106.

Gupta, S.P. , Dalal K, Nanji, R, Dandekar, A., Bomble, S., Mushrif-Tripathy V., Kadgaonkar S., Chaudhari, G., Sharma P. and Abbas, R. 2005. Preliminary Report of the third Season of Excavations at Sanjan- 2004. *Journal of Indian Ocean Archaeology 2:* 55-61.

Handa, D. M.K.Gupta . 2003. Some More Kalchuri Coins, in *IIRNS NEWSLINE,* issue 39 (Amiteshwar Jha Ed.), pp.3-4. Nasik –Anjaneri.

Mirashi V. 1962. A Coin of Jayāśraya , *Studies in Indology,* Vol. III. University of Nagpur , pp. 118 - 120.

Motichandra . 2010 . *Sārthavāha* , Sahitya Akademi, New Delhi , pp. 254 -255.

Nanji, Rukhsana and Homi Dhalla 2007. The landing of the Zoroastrians in Sanjan: The Archaeological evidence. In Parsis in India and the Diaspora (Hinnels, J. and Williams, A. ed.) Routledge South Asian Religion Studies: London. 35-58.

Nanji, Rukshana 2011. *Mariners and Merchants: A Study of the ceramics from Sanjan (Gujarat)*. BAR International Series 2231 (Sanjan Report Volume 1), 241 pp.

A Report on the Sculptures from Sanjan, 2004

Shivendra B. Kadgaonkar

This paper presents a preliminary survey of the sculptures found during exploration at Sanjan in 2004.

The ancient site of Sanjan was excavated by the WZCF from year 2002 to 2004. Sanjan is in Tal. Umbargaon, Dist. Valsad, State. Gujarat. Sanjan is situated on the northern bank of the Varoli River. Sculptures found at Sanjan during the exploration are located in different places. These stone sculptures are broken and eroded but comparatively in good condition. In the sense their features, their symbols can be easily identified. All the sculptures are lying in natural condition without any evidence of modification or decoration. Visitors to Sanjan in the past have also noted the existence of sculptures and idols at the site. Gazetteer of Bombay presidency vol. xiv (1882) mentions undulating landscape with remains of brick structures, sculptures & architectural remains. It mentions sculptural fragments outside a village home near peer-no-kuvo at Sanjan. Ibn Haukal, the Arab traveler who visited to Sanjan in the 10th century A.D. mentions a Jama Masjid & an idol and a temple.

The sculptural remains observed at Sanjan during explorations are listed below:

1. Devi = This sculpture is lying flat on the ground and is broken at middle. This sculpture was found in a nearby water tank by villagers. The Devi sculpture depicts her in a seating position. She is wearing ornaments like mala (necklace), a big round shaped earrings, keyura (armlets), anklet and karandaka mukuta (type of crown). She is wearing a uttariya. Her right hand is in varada mudra and holding aksha-mala. Aksha-mala is a symbol of Goddess Saraswati or Goddess Brahmani. It may be concluded that the Devi figure may belong to one of these two Goddesses.

Devi

59

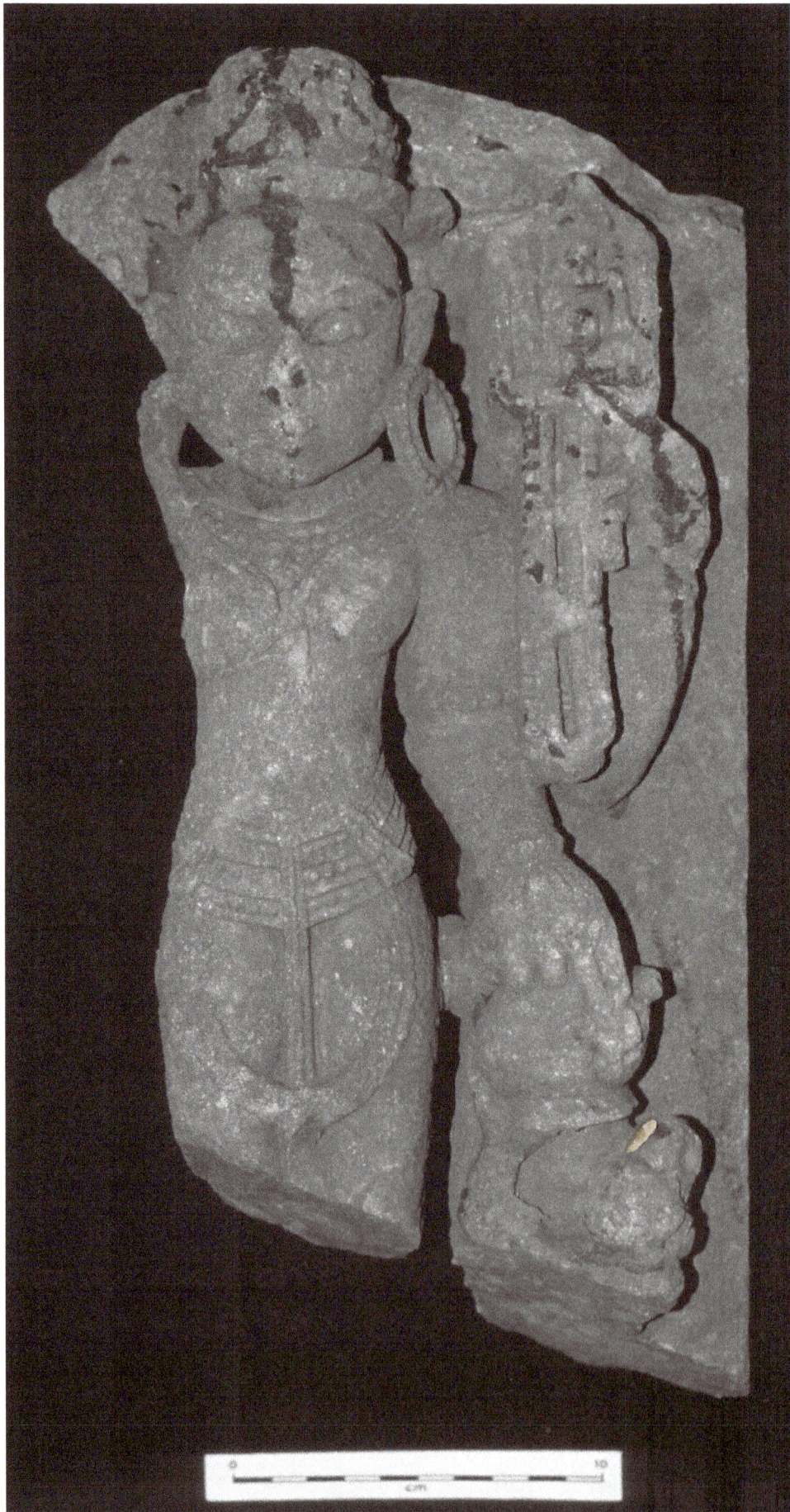

Goddess Parvati

God Shiva or Shankara

2. Parvati = The sculpture of Goddess Parvati is a standing figure in good condition. She has four hands though her legs and two hands on the right side are broken. In her upper left hand she holds a Ganesha figure and another hand holds a Kamandlu or sacred water pot. She is wearing a mala around neck, a big round earrings, bangles, waist-band and mukuta. Her fish shaped eyes are quite noticeable.

3. Shiva = The shiva figure is much weathered and its legs,and hands are broken. His jata or matted locks is a prominent looking feature. He is wearing a dhoti . His facial features are not visible due to erosion. The figure is in standing posture.

4. Kubera = This sculpture of God of the wealth, Kubera was found in a cultivated field. This figure is open to the sky. Kubera is seated in a Lalitasana . He has a pot-belly, which is his charecteristic. He is wearing a uttariya, sacred thread and an anklet around left foot. In his left hand he is holding a mongoose shaped bag which is his symbol. The mouth of the bag is open with coins spilling out. The head and right hand of this figure are missing.

5. Gajathara sculpture = A fragment of Gajathara (elephant moulding) is lying under one roof behind Mazdarise Apartments in Sanjan town. 'Gaja' in Sanskrit means elephant. Here elephants are shown from the front. This fragment has remains with six elephants. Their trunks, big ears, head and legs are properly shown and clearly

seen. Next to this, a Narathara fragment (moulding with human figures) can be seen. 'Nara' in Sanskrit means male. In this fragment males are shown in war scene.

6. Chamaradharini = Chamaradharini in Sanskrit means a woman holding a fly whisk. This tiny figure is lying , a little away from Gajathara and Narathara. She is seen holding in her right hand a chamar or chavri. She wears a mala around her neck. Her eyes,both hands, head and hairdo can be clearly seen. Her legs are broken.

7. Chandrashila = A fragment of Chandarshila stone can see on the northern bank of the Varoli River behind the school at Sanjan. In this sculpture both sides of shankha or conch a lotus buds are shown. Chandrashila in Sanskrit means moon-shaped stone.

8. Temple Pillar = A fragment of a temple pillar is kept in W. Z. O's Wadia Sanatorium premises in Sanjan town. This fragment is in good condition. Besides this some other temple fragments also lying scattered in Sanjan village.

Conclusion

Several inscriptions attest to the antiquity of Sanjan and the settlement in ancient times. The Nagarjunakonda inscription of Abhira Vasusena, Year 30 which has been dated by D.C Sircar to c. 278 A.D, the Nahapana inscription of cave no.10, Pandulena (Nasik) mentioning Nanangola (Nargol, in the vicinity of Sanjan) dated to *c.*32 A.D – 77 A.D,

61

Kubera (God of Wealth)

Gajathara

Charmardharini (A Lady with Flywhisk)

Chandrashila (Moon Stone)

Narathara

Sanjan copper plates of Buddhavarsa (671 A.D) found at Umbargaon and Amoghavarsa I copper plates dated to 871 A.D giving the administrative extent of Sanjan are some of the epigraphic sources which confirm the existence of Sanjan in the early centuries of the Christian Era.

From the copper plates found at Chinchani (Tal. Dahanu, Dist. Thane) we came to know that saniyana or samyana which is modern sanjan was ruled by Rashtrakuta kings followed by the Silahara dynasty. Rashtrakuta king Krishnaraja (878 A.D. to 915 A.D.) handed over Sanjan mandala or province to muslim Tajik governer Muhammad Sugatipa. His sanskritized name was Madhumati .

He gave grants to mathika (monastery) and for offering naivedya & dipotsava to the goddess Dasami (mother goddess Durga or Parvati). Though a muslim ruler he patronized Hindu temples and even invited north Indian Brahmins to settle here. Rashtrakutas ruled this province or mandala for nearly four centuries (c.700 A.D to 1000 A.D). The copper plate grant of Krishna III (939 A.D to 967 A.D.) mentions a legal dispute between the devotees of God Bhillamaladeva and the goddess. This was about a piece of land in Sanjan.

The above discussion shows that the sculptures presently found at Sanjan during exploration may be part or fragments of a big temple complex which was dedicated to either god Bhillmaladeva or Goddess Dasami. The period of these sculptures is between 5th - 6th century A.D. to 12th – 13th century A.D. This chronology is hypothesized on the basis of style and art and corroborative evidence such as inscriptional and numismatic finds pertaining to this site. It proves that Hindu culture was predominant in Sanjan before the arrival of the Parsis. These sculptures give major support to the inscriptional evidence of temples at Sanjan. Gajathara, Narathara and Chandra shila are the important sculptural fragments of temple complex from Silahara period. gajathara and narathara are the bands of elephants and males on the plinth of temple. Their importance in temple architecture is to carry the load of the huge temple structure. Chandrashila is a moon-shaped stone which is placed at the main entrance of the temple. However, the earliest sculptural evidence at Sanjan is provided by the Kubera figure which can be dated to approximately the 2nd or 3rd century A.D on stylistic basis.

Here it would not be amiss to mention that in the year 2004 excavations at Sanjan Bandar (SJN – B), in the lower strata, a small terracotta Ganesha figure was recovered. It is the size of betel nut. Even though a small figurine, the Ekdanta (single tusk) of this Ganesha can easily noticed. It should also be mentioned that two shards of Red Polished Ware retrieved in the first season of excavations at Sanjan are indicative of an earlier settlement in or around Sanjan. They add to the evidence provided by the inscriptions and the sculptural remains that an early settlement at Sanjan predated the arrival of the migrant community of the Parsis.

The above sculptures support inscriptional and literary evidence for the existence of a temple at Sanjan in the ancient past.

A planned excavation and exploration is needed to locate the temple complex at Sanjan.

Acknowledgments

The author would like to acknowledge Dr. Homi Dhalla of the WZCF who gave permission for writing of this report on sculptures. Thanks to (Late) Dr. S.P. Gupta, Director of excavations and Dr. Kurush Dalal for giving me an opportunity to participate in the excavation and exploration. Special thanks to Dr. Rukshana Nanji for support.

My deep gratitude to Dr. G.B. Deglurkar (Chancellor of Deccan college, (Deemed University) Post-graduate Research Institute for Archaeology, Pune) for his valuable suggestions on this topic.

References

Gupta S.P. (et.al) 2005. Preliminary Report of the third season of Excavations at Sanjan – 2004 . in Journal of Indian Ocean Archaeology, no. 2. New Delhi.

Joshi N.P. 1979. Bhartiya Murtishastra (in Marathi) , Maharashtra vidyapeeth grantha nirmiti mandal, Nagpur-1

Khare G.H. 1939. Murti vidnyan (in Marathi), Bharta Itihas Samshodhak Mandal , Pune 30

Nanji Rukshana. J (2007), The Study of Early Medieval Ceramics in India, with Special Reference to Sanjan (Gujrat). Unpublished Ph.D Thesis Submitted to Deccan College (Deemed University) Pune.

Sankalia H. D. 1983 Sanjan – A Miniature Bombay in c.A.D. 980 in SRI DINESACANDRIKA , studies in Indology. SHRI D.C. SIRCAR FESTSCHRIFT . Sundeep prakashan, Delhi.

A Report on the Molluscan Shell Remains from Sanjan Excavations (2002-2004)

Arati Deshpande-Mukherjee

Dept. of Archaeology,
Deccan College, Pune.
Email: arati_d_m@hotmail.com

This report deals with the study of molluscan shell remains recovered from the excavations at the coastal site of Sanjan on the Gujarat coast. This site (N 20 11'59.6; E 72 48'00.2) is situated in Umargaon taluka, District Valsad in Gujarat. It is spread over an area approximately 2 km x 0.75 km. and is located on the left bank of the Vairoli creek. Reference to Sanjan was made first in the persian poem Kisse-I-Sanjan written by a Parsi priest Dastur Boman Kaikobad in approximately 1600 AD. (Edulji 1991). This is probably the only document which tells us about the Parsis exodus into India after fleeing from Iran due to islamic persecution. It is at this place that the Parsis first settled down after arriving in India. Hence excavations at Sanjan were primarily carried out to establish the existence and location of the ancient settlement along with the cultural activities at the site. It was excavated for three seasons (2002-2004) by the Indian Archaeological Society and World Zarathusti Cultural foundation. A large number of artefacts, and structural remains were recovered. On their basis the site is dated between the 8th and 13th centuries AD. (Gupta et.al 2002, 2003, 2004).

In addition the three season excavations at Sanjan (2002-2004) have also yielded an apprieciable number of molluscan shells along with ceramics, glass, copper objects, human and animal skeletal remains. A detailed study of the recovered shell material was carried out in order to determine the origins and role of molluscs in the cultural history of the site.

Shell Analysis

The shell analysis was carried out at the archaeozoology laboratory of the Deccan College, Pune. The shells were subjected to both wet and dry cleaning. Care was taken while cleaning the shells because of their fragile condition.Taphonomic observations such as charring, breakage, perforation, modification, discolouration, abrasion, dissolution, etc. were carried out. Dimensional measurements of the shells were taken. Shell identification was carried out to the possible species level by referring to the reference collection at the Deccan College and by consulting published literature (Apte 1998).

The shell Samples from the following three locations were studied (a) Mound SJN- B (Bandar), (b) SJN-D (from inside the Bhandar in the Dhakma area) and (c) Mound SJN-K (Kolikhadi).

(1) Mound SJN-B (Bandar) is along the Vairoli river and is severely eroded because of flooding during the monsoon seasons. It is the site of the creek port that had served as the main settlement at Sanjan This has revealed a large number of brick structures. The structures were exposed by scraping and yielded artefacts and ceramics. A trench designated TT3 was taken on the embankment overlooking the creek. In this remains of a square well were revealed. Trench TT4 in 2004 was taken slightly away from the embankment in the same area. Shells were recovered along with ceramics from trench TT1, TT2 and TT4.

(2) The Bhandar in the Dakhma mound (SJN-D)

This lies at the confluence of the Koli Khadi and the Tukkar Nala. According to the local tradition it was a 'bhastu' a local word for a Parsi tower of silence or Dakhma. Excavations revealed a structure made up of three distinct parts. One of the parts, a brick lined dry well constitutes the Bhandar. It is almost 90 cm. deep and approximately 5 m. in diameter and lies on the virgin soil. It has an inner facing of seven courses of bricks, the lowest is indented and very carefully plastered with lime. Excavations within the Bhandar have revealed a large number of human skeletal remains. A few shells were recovered from trench OX1 which were taken up for identification. These are mainly belonging to the terrestrial gastropod Cyclophorus indicus.

(3) Mound SJN-K (Kolikhadi)

The second seasons excavation 2003 was carried out on the left bank of the Kolikhadi and was designated SJN-K. It is a high long oval shaped mound, roughly 50 m. long, N-S, and is 30 m. wide, E-W. It is separated from the neighbouring mound by a deep rain gully. Four layers were revealed layers 1 and 2 were habitational layers while layer 3 was the natural soil on which the settlement was established. The total habitation deposit was about a metre. **Layer 1** was the uppermost layer, brown in colour, with numerous brickbats and bricklets interspersed through it. It is quite disturbed and its thickness varied from 10-15 cm. **Layer 2** is reddish brown in colour ranging in thickness from 18-41 cm. A number of brickbats, brick and stone structures were visible here. In this layer burials HS-1/2/3 and 4 were found. The ceramics present were coarse and slipped Red and Grey wares while grey wares are almost absent. Other objects found were coins and beads. **Layer 3** is a dark brown clayey layer and is the natural soil on which the settlement was first established. Its thickness varies from 5 to 35cm. **Layer 4** is the virgin soil which is a yellowish sandy layer interspersed with small kankar nodules and decomposed marine shells. The artefacts recovered from SJN-K comprised a large number of beads (n 427), glass bangle fragments, terracotta discs, stone artefacts like a rotary quern and coins. Shells were recovered from trenches A3, B4 and B5,

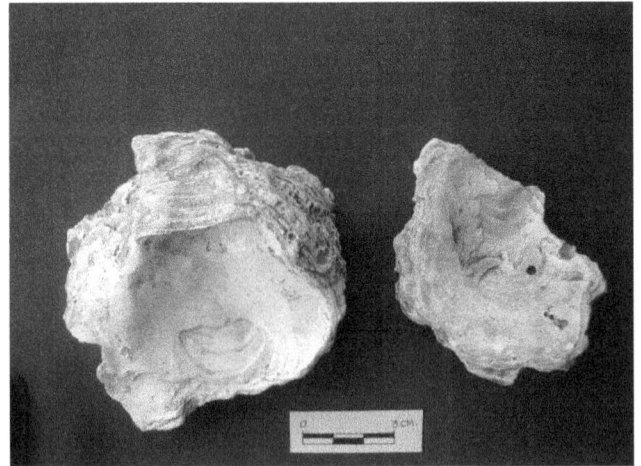

Fig.1 Shells of Oyster species Crassostrea gryphoides

Results

From a total of 197 shells studied, 17 molluscan species are identified while a few could not be identified because of their small size and discolouration due to weathering (Table 1.) All are marine in origin except for one terrestrial gastropod. Bivalve shells are greater in number as compared to those of gastropods. In the entire assemblage, oyster shells are predominant. The overall shell preservation is poor with a high rate of fragmentation. A majority of the shells are fragile, have lost their outer shell layer and have a chalky white appearance. The surface examination of the shells revealed very few traces of human modification like perforation, abrasion, breakage patterns, etc. However, to a certain extent some amount of human activity is indicated by the presence of a few cut and charred shells. Some of the important species represented in the collection are

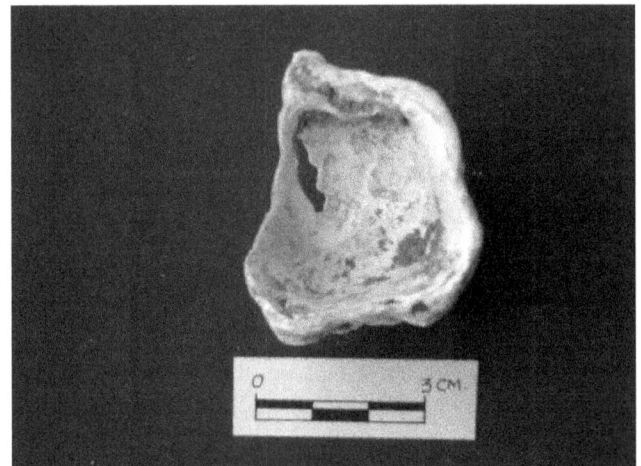

Fig 2. Shell of rock oyster Crasssostrea cucullata

1. *Crassostrea sp.*

The most commonly occurring shells at Sanjan are those of the oyster belonging to the genus *Crassostrea*. Two species of this genus *Crassostrea gryphoides* and *Crassostrea cucullata* have been identified in the collection of which the former shows maximum representation. Mostly fragmented shells of *C. gryphoides* having a chalky appearance were found while few fragments indicate exposure to fire and are bluish grey in colour.

As compared to other bivalves and gastropods, oysters are sessile and are found attached to a substratum like rocks and mangroves in the mudflats of the intertidal zone. They also occur at the mouth of estuaries and backwaters. *Crassostrea gryphoides* has a broad, roundish, laminated shell, narrow in the anterior margin and broader in the posterior margin (Fig. 1). The upper valve is thin, flat and opercular while lower valve is thick. It has a prominent central groove with elevations in the sides on the hinge of the left valve. The entire inner surface is white and glossy. The adductor muscle scar is oblong and pearly white (Rao 1974).

2. *Crassostrea cucullata* is smaller in size as compared to

Fig 3. Sawn perforated apex of Turbinella pyrum *shell*

C. gryphoides. Its shell is trigonal, slightly oblong with a thick lower valve and a flat upper valve (Fig. 2). The margin of the shell is thrown into folds. It is found firmly attached to rocks in the intertidal zone as well as on rocks in an open coast where both temperature and salinity are high. Both *C. gryphoides* and *C. cucullata* are very common along the Indian west coast.

3. *Nerita* sp. Two species belonging to the genus Nerita occur as mostly complete shells and are discoloured because of weathering. They are Nerita sp. and Nerita crepidularia (Fig. 6). The former could not be identified to the species level. The shells do not show any traces of human modification and were naturally incorporated. These are small gastropod shells that are very common along the west coast. The shells are thick with a depressed spire, mouth is ovate or horseshoe shaped. On the shell surface, dark dots are visible. These range in size from 15-20 mm. and live on rocks and mudflats in the intertidal zone and mangrove areas. These are well adapted to a brackish water habitat (Apte 1998). Dead shells are often found on the sandy beaches along the Konkan coast.

4. *Meretrix meretrix, Anadara* sp. *Trachycardium* sp. *Tapes* sp. A few small complete to broken shells of all these marine bivalves are present (Fig. 7). These are also found in large numbers inhabiting the intertidal and estuarine sand/ mud flats along the Konkan and the Gujarat coast.

5. *Turbinella pyrum* commonly referred to as the sacred Indian Chank is a large marine gastropod shell ranging in size from 90-200 mm. In India Its occurrence is restricted to the Gujarat coast mainly in the Gulf of Kachchh and the south eastern coast ie. the Tamil Nadu coast. At Sanjan, a total of n= 22 T. pyrum fragments were obtained mainly from the Bandar area (Tr.TT2, TT4) and the Kolikhadi area (Tr. B4 & B5). These like the other shells are also weathered and show shell dissolution. T.pyrum is represented by fragments from its main whorl, apex region and the central columella. Many of these indicate sawing (Fig. 3, 4, 5). However no complete shells, bangles or other objects made from it were recovered.

6. *Pugilina buchephala* is represented by a single columella which is highly weathered with a chalky appearance. This is also a large marine gastropod found in tidal mudflats in the intertidal zone.

7. *Cypraea sp.* three species of the genus commonly referred to as cowries have been identified 1) *Erosaria lamarcki, 2) Moneta moneta* and 3*) Cypraea sp.* From SJN-B

Locus B, Tr. TT4. Depth 3.42m, sealing Layer (2) a complete shell of *Erosaria lamarcki* having a Length of 20.13 mm. was found. It was probably exposed to fire hence brownish in colour.

8. *Oliva* sp. a single complete shell of this particular marine gastropod having a length of 25.32 mm. with its

Fig 4. Sawn columella of Turbinella pyrum

Fig 5. Sawn basal portion of the main shell whorl of Turbinella pyrum

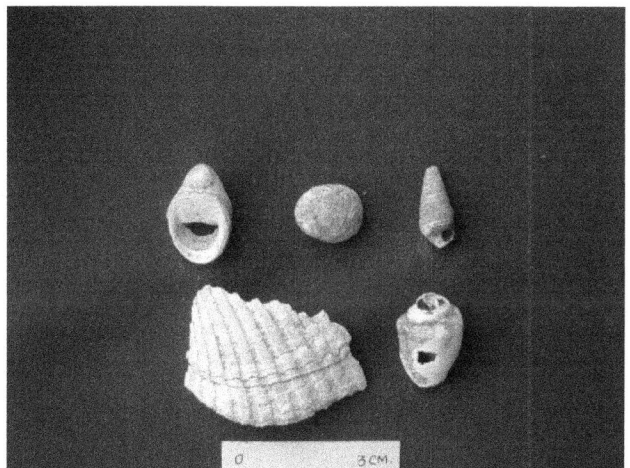

Fig 6. Assorted marine shells. Top row left to right Nerita crepidularia, Nerita sp. and Cerithidae sp.; bottom row left to right Trachycardium sp. and Cantharus sp.

apex perforated was found from SJN–B, Tr. TT2, Depth 1.42 m., layer (3). (Fig. 7). Shells belongng to the family Olividae are found on sand flats in the intertidal zone. *Oliva* shells have been reported from some of the Harappan sites in Gujarat and Chalcolithic sites in Maharashtra like Inamgaon, Chandoli and Nevasa (Deshpande-Mukherjee 1998, 2005, 2006-7). At these sites the shells had been used as beads by perforating the apex.

9. *Cyclophorus indicus* At Sanjan complete and broken shells of the terristrial gastropod Cyclophorus indicus were recovered only from within the Bhandar in the Dakhma area (Fig. 8). The shell measurements indicate that a majority were adult sized shells The shell has a large main body whorl with a pointed apex and a thin shell. On its outer surface faint brownish decorations are visible. This is a land snail which is found inhabiting areas with high humidity and vegetation.

Discussion

The excavations at Sanjan have revealed a fairly wide range of molluscan species (Table 1). These mainly belong to a marine estuarine habitat except for one species, which is a terrestrial gastropod. In the overall shell assemblage, a general absence of freshwater molluscs is observed. Majority of the shells show poor preservation, which is attributed to post-depositional processes. It is observed that shell dissolution was largely responsible for the chalky appearance and deterioration of the shells. Additional factors such as biogenic activities, erosion, flooding and water logging of some parts of the site like the Bandar area have also been instrumental in the bad preservation of the shells.

Both natural as well as anthropogenic processes were responsible for introducing various molluscan shells into the deposit at Sanjan. Natural processes and nearness to the shore had introduced many of the species which did not have any particular role to play at the site. These comprised small sized molluscs such as *Nerita* sp., *Nerita crepidularia, Cypraea* sp. and *Cerithidae* sp. As these had inhabited the nearby tidal mudflats, they were probably brought to the site accidentally as a result of activity by humans, birds, tidal waves, etc. In case of the shells of the terristrial gastropod *Cyclophorus* which were found only inside the Bhandar in the Dakhma area, these were also naturally introduced. Their depth wise representation shows the continuous occupation of the Bhandar area by them in the past. These represent a once living shell assemblage, which because of their short lifespan got deposited after their death. It is quite likely that the lime plastering within the Bhandar had attracted these snails since they require calcium carbonate to build their shells. Most terrestrial gastropods thrive in areas with lime rich soils, thick vegetation and wet humid conditions.

Occurrence of certain species like Crassostrea, Meretrix meretrix, Anadara sp., Turbinella pyrum, Oliva sp. and

Fig 7. Assorted marine shells; left to right: Anadara *sp.,* Cerithium *sp. and* Oliva *sp.*

Fig 8. Terristrial gastropod shells of Cyclophorus indicus

Cypraea sp. in the Bandar and Kolikhadi areas reveals their intentional exploitation by the Sanjan inhabitants. Both these areas had served as the habitation areas where a wide range of activities had been performed. The main purpose of exploiting these molluscs was for both as a dietary resource and in shell working. Predominance of oyster shells in these areas reveals their dietary use. Their utilisation was more as compared to other molluscs like Meretrix meretrix and Anadara sp.

Molluscs especially oysters are well known for their food value both in the past as well as in the present. Along the west coast today these along with clams form important commercial shellfisheries and are brought to Mumbai for sale (Deshpande-Mukherjee 2000). At Sanjan in addition

Table 1. Molluscs identified in SJN-B (Bandar), SJN-K (Kolikhadi) and SJN-D (Dakhma) area

No:	Species	Family	M/BV/G	SJN-B	SJN-K	SJN-D
1	Crassostrea gryphoides	Osteridae	M/BV	63	5	6
2	Crassostrea cucullata	Osteridae	M/BV	1	0	
3	Meretrix meretrix	Veneridae	M/BV	8	0	
4	Cypraea sp.	Cypraeidae	M/G	1	0	
5	Erosaria lamarcki	Cypraeidae	M/G	2	0	
6	Moneta moneta	Cypraeidae	M/G	0	1	
7	Nerita crepidularia	Neritidae	M/G	0	4	
8	Nerita sp.	Neritidae	M/G	4	2	
9	Turbinella pyrum	Turbinellidae	M/G	6	16	
10	Pugilna buchephala	Melongenidae	M/G	1	0	
11	Anadara sp.	Arcidae	M/BV	9	0	
12	Oliva sp.	Olividae	M/G	1	0	
13	Cerithidae sp.	Potamidiae	M/G	1	0	
14	Cyclophorus indicus	Cyclophoridae	T/G	0	0	20
15	Trachycardium sp.	Cardiidae	M/BV	6	0	
16	Tapes sp.	Veneridae	M/BV	1	0	
17	Cantharus sp.	Buccinidae	M/G	1	0	
18	Unidentified marine bivalve	Unknown	M/BV	5	4	
19	Unidentified marine gastropod	Unknown	M/G	4	5	
20	Unidentified shell fragments				20	
	Total NISP			*114*	*57*	*26*

M-Marine; **T**-terristrial; **BV**-Bivalve; **G**-Gastropod

to fish and terrestrial mammals, molluscs especially oysters had also made significant contribution to the food economy.

Due to their easy availability and food value, these may have served as a commonly exploited food resource. Proximity to the nearby estuary and mudflats along the shore had enabled the site inhabitants to regularly collect oysters and other molluscs. In these areas, oyster beds are found spread over a large area hence a large-scale collection is possible. By handpicking at low tide these could be easily collected when they got exposed. C. gryphoides being fairly big sized can be easily dislodged from the mangroves, rocks and mudflats. After collection these were brought to the site for consumption. Present-day procurement techniques involve detaching oysters from rocks using a sharp instrument and then putting them into bags or aluminum vessels (Deshpande-Mukherjee 2000). Meat extraction is done at the settlements by shucking, a technique that involves inserting a knife between the two valves and opening the shells. At Sanjan similar method along with roasting and steaming might have been employed for meat removal. In the case of the rock oyster C. cucullata, meat extraction was probably done at the procurement source itself, as it is difficult to detach these particular shells from the rocks. Hence its limited occurance at the settlement

Apart from a dietary use, shells were probably used for obtaining lime. Molluscan shells are a good source of lime due to their rich calcium carbonate content. However it is difficult to identify this aspect in the archaeological

record since the lime making process involves complete destruction of the shells. As a result very little evidence is left behind. However at Sanjan in some of the structures like the Bhandar, in the Dakhma area, a close examination of the lime plastering has indicated the use of shell lime by the traces of calcined shells in it. A regular collection of oysters for dietary purpose might have ensured a good supply of shells for lime making as well. Shell lime was probably used for both domestic purpose as well as in the Dakhma area in the disposal of the dead. In recent times, lime manufacture using discarded oyster and other molluscan shells is still practised on a limited scale along the Konkan coast (Deshpande-Mukherjee 2000).

Another important aspect revealed from the shell study is the evidence for shell working. Although no shell objects were found but presence of sawn Turbinella pyrum shell fragments mainly from the Bandar and Kolikhadi area have indicated this particular activity. Generally occurrence of similar types of cut shells at most archaeological sites in India is found to be indicative of shell working associated with the manufacture of shell bangles. The T. pyrum fragments from Sanjan closely resemble the shell debitage observed in the shellcutting workshops in present day West Bengal which have resulted during bangle production (Deshpande-Mukherjee 2006). Hence from their study it is assumed that some amount of shell working had been carried out at Sanjan. This had probably involved the manufacture of shell bangles and other objects. However considering the absence of finished shell objects, the available shell evidence and limited nature of the excavation, it is difficult to find out the nature and extent of this particular activity at the site. Here further detailed investigations are required for confirming this aspect. Chank shell bangle production was very common in peninsular India till the Historic period after which a slow decline is observed (Deshpande-Mukherjee 2008). Hence this shell evidence from Sanjan is important as it reveals shell working activity even during the medieval period, evidence for which is otherwise scarce in this particular period. So far this is observed at only a few sites such as Nevasa in this region.

Besides elucidating the cultural role of the shells, appreciable information regarding the immediate local environment at the time of occupation could be inferred from the different molluscs present. The present-day habitat of the recovered shell assemblage indicates a molluscan fauna, which is typical of estuaries and creeks along this coast. Some of the species like Crassostrea, Oliva, Meretrix, Anadara, Nerita are still found to inhabit similar habitats. This in a way suggests that no major shoreline changes have occurred. Presence of estuarine conditions and occurrence of tidal mudflats with mangroves in the past are hinted at through the presence of oysters shells, Nerita crepidularia and Erosaria lamarcaki. Occurrence of oysters also indicates brackish water conditions. Further existence of wet humid conditions along with good vegetation is revealed through the presence of Cyclophorus shells. Today on the west coast, Cyclophorous is found in groups inhabiting cool areas like rock crevices and the root of trees and bushes. These favour high rainfall and thick vegetation. Similar species have been sighted on the floors of some of the coastal forts like Janjira, Korlai on the Konkan coast (personal observations). Unfortunately very little is known about the ecology and biology of terrestrial gastropods in India.

Thus the overall shell study has helped to identify the role played by various molluscs in the cultural history of the site at Sanjan. Inspite of its coastal location, the overall pattern of molluscan usage is fairly limited. This may be partly due to poor preservation as well as because of socio-religious attitudes prevalent then which might have restricted the use of molluscs. However both dietary and industrial use to a certain extent are indicated. This has helped gain some insights into the local subsistence pattern and palaeoeconomy of the Sanjan inhabitants

Acknowledgements

I wish to thank the Late Dr.S.P.Gupta and his team, Dr. Homi Dhalla and the Zarushtra trust, Mumbai for inviting me to study the material. I also offer my sincere acknowledgments to Drs Kurush Dalal, Abhijeet Dandekar and Rukshana Nanji for involving me in the project.

References

Apte, D. 1998. The book of Indian Shells. Bombay Natural History Society.Mumbai: Oxford University Press.

Deshpande Mukherjee A. 1998. Shell fishing and Shell craft Activities during the Harappan period in Gujarat. *Man and Environment* Vol XXXIII (1): 63-81

Deshpande-Mukherjee, A. 2000. An Ethnographic Account of Contemporary Shellfish Gathering on the Konkan Coast, Maharashtra. Man and Environment XXV (2): 79-92.

Deshpande-Mukherjee, A. 2005. Marine Shell Utilisation by the Chalcolithic Socities of the Western Deccan region of India in Archaeomalacology :Molluscs in Former Environments of Human Behaviou, (Daniella E.Bar-Yosef Mayer Ed.),pp. 174-184, Oxbow Books.

Deshpande-Mukherjee, A. 2006. Reconstructing the Past: Ethnographic Observations on Shellworking at Bishnupur. In Gautam Sengupta, Suchira Roychoudhury and Sujit Som (Eds.) Past and Present: Ethnoarchaeology in India, pp. 383-409, New Delhi and Centre for Archaeological Studies and Training Eastern India: Pragati Publications.

Deshpande-Mukherjee, A. 2006-7. Marine Molluscs at Ancient Settlements in the Deccan. *Bulletin of the Deccan College* 66-67: 259-283.

Deshpande-Mukherjee. A. 2008 Archaeomalacological Research in India with Special Reference to the Early Historic Exploitation of the Sacred Conch Shell Turbinella pyrum in the Western Deccan. in Early Human Impact on Megamolluscs (Andrzej Antczak and Roberto Ciprani eds.), pp.209-222. BAR British Archaeological Series 1865 Oxford.

Edulji, H. 1991. Kissseh-i-Sanjan, Bombay: K.R.Cama Oriental Institute, Mumbai.

Gupta, S.P., K.F. Dalal, A. Dandekar, R. Nanji, R. Mitra and R. Pandey 2002. A Prelimnary Report on the Excavations at Sanjan (2002), Puratattva 32:182-198.

Gupta, S.P., K.F. Dalal, A. Dandekar, R. Nanji, P. Aravazhi and S. Bomble 2004. On the footsteps of Zoroastrian Parsis in India. Excavations at Sanjan on the West Coast-2003. Journal of Indian Ocean Archaeology 1:93-106.

Gupta, S.P., K.F. Dalal, R. Nanji, A. Dandekar S. Bomble, V. Mushriff-Tripathi, S. Kadgaoncar, G. Chaudhuri, Pranab Sharma and Riza Abbas 2005. Prelimnary Report of the Third Season of Excavations at Sanjan-2004. Indian Ocean Archaeology No:2: 55-61.

Rao, K.S.1974. Edible bivalves:Mussels and Oysters. In R.V.Nair and K.S. Rao (Eds.) Commercial Molluscs of India, pp. 4-39. Cochin: Central Marine Fisheries Research Institute.

www.ingramcontent.com/pod-product-compliance
Lightning Source LLC
Chambersburg PA
CBHW061304270326
41932CB00029B/3475